PRAISES
CLOSING IS NOT YOUR PROBLEM!

"Increase your revenues, build a sales team that consistently hits quotes and be able to identify the true cause of sales failure. *Closing is NOT Your Problem!* is the leader's guide to building an unstoppable sales team, real closers!"

—Monte Holm,
Co-Founder World Financial Group

"Using the information in this book, I have continued to expand no matter what is happening with the economy. Having a sales technology that is effective for me and my entire team no matter what challenges the environment brings. Each aspect of this book is centered around getting results and improving skills. This book is a vital tool for success!"

—Michael Coleman,
CEO Dynamic Expansion Financial Services

"The book is amazing and a BIG MEAL. I am learning virtually on every page."

—Marshall Goldberg,
Technology Industry Evangelist

"I've read hundreds of books over my career and this book is different! I've highlighted, circled, underlined and scribbled notes in this book. This is the kind of book that you will want to read again and again!

—Ken Porter, Co-Founder & CEO SAVVI

"Finally someone broke down the simplicity of the sales process and put the building blocks together in a way that will effectively change the way selling is done. Great research and focus on where sales are broken, and how to improve conversion rates rather than working harder. A game changer for sales management! "

—Todd Supplee,
Entertainment Industry Executive Partner

"If you want to create a sales focused organization where every seller is a closer then this book is a must read. The authors have managed to bring to light a better way to educate and enable a sales focused organization where every seller is a producer of revenue."

—Zane Adam, Technology Industry V.P.

"*Closing is NOT Your Problem!* is an outstanding book. It covers all aspects of a sale in a unique way; mindset, approach, trust and the close. A must-read to help you find more success in business…and in life!"

—Curt Braken, Business Entrepreneur

"I've been working to crack the mysteries of selling for a very long time. This book with its illustrations has given me a transformational understanding of sales and what it really means to help your client or customer."

—Bayou Bennett, 50x Award Winning Filmmaker

"I have run my own technology business for over three decades and have read many business books especially on the topic of selling. Many of these books are written in a lofty manner with little value offered to the reader but *Closing is NOT Your Problem!* is the exact opposite. This is the first fully illustrated easy to understand guide, packed with the required fundamentals to be successful in selling anything. I really like the explanation and illustrations provided in Chapter 2: The Sales Process. The way the information is provided sheds new light on how to run an effective sales process including what to do with those leads not ready to buy. This book should be one handed to every salesperson in your company and told to read it at least twice a year. If you do this you should see your revenue grow magically."

—Scott Kriesberg,
Technology Industry CEO and Author

CLOSING
is NOT your
PROBLEM!

Very best,

Nick

CLOSING
is NOT your
PROBLEM!

How Can You CLOSE A Door
That Was NEVER OPENED?

Nick & Lisa Terrenzi
The FIRST Fully Illustrated Guide to Selling!

Published by:
8020 Sales Technologies

Printed in the United States of America

ISBN: 978-1-7364805-0-2 (paperback)
ISBN: 978-1-7364805-1-9 (ebook)

Book Design: Creative Publishing Book Design
Illustrator: Jaclyn Nelson

DEDICATION

This is the first fully illustrated guide to selling. A selling handbook with real solutions that work. We want to help individuals confidently and competently sell themselves, their ideas, their visions, their dreams, their products, and/or their services. We want to help individuals positively impact themselves, their families, their associates, and their company, thereby positively impacting the overall economy.

We hereby dedicate this book to:

1. The millions of business owners and executives building sales teams. We hope you can use the information to solve the common problem of 80/20 (80% of sales done by 20% of salespeople) within your company!

2. To the millions of sales and customer service people worldwide who want to consistently sell and be successful! We know you want to help and have a successful career in sales. Our purpose with this book is to provide you with technology that you can immediately apply and get results, getting your career on track or taking it to a whole new level!

3. To the millions of customers with prior bad buying experiences. We aim to revolutionize the sales and customer service industry. All of us need a Professional to answer our questions and guide us safely through the sales/buying process.

4. And finally, we dedicate this book to the best friend and salesperson we ever trained. Holleigh Taufer Gregorian, you left this earth way too early but your influence on life lives on in all of us. This is for you Hol.

TABLE OF CONTENTS

PREFACE
from Nick and Lisa

This book is our first collaboration on a subject we've extensively researched together: the 80/20 rule. That is, 80 percent of sales are produced by the top 20 percent of salespeople and executives in most businesses. Given the fact that the 80/20 rule continues to be a worldwide problem in businesses, we decided to work together to research, discover the solution, and re-engineer the sales process.

After more than five years of global research and billions of dollars in sales, we discovered the exact skills possessed by the top 20 percent of salespeople in the world—those professionals responsible for 80 percent of sales. We discovered what causes most salespeople to be inconsistent and fail to achieve their quotas. Using our research, we were able to create new technology. This started to solve the 80/20 problem. The result is a new set of sales standards!

During our research project, we found that while there were ideas, books, systems, funnels, closing programs, and knowledge, no one had brought all these components together. Thus, there was not a complete "technology" that had been developed for sales. Without exact technology to follow, sales failures could not be scientifically detected and resolved. This was a major reason for the 80/20 problem. Technology per the definition includes making, modification, usage, and knowledge of tools, machines, techniques, crafts, systems, and methods of organization.

Through all of our research, we realized that the problem itself had been seriously underestimated. This resulted in solutions that did not fully address the magnitude of the problem. We realized that it would take uncompromising dedication to create a complete solution for the 80/20 problem. SELLability Technologies is focused on the science of development and selling of solutions, and the practical application of those solutions, successfully solving the 80/20 problem.

The solutions include re-engineering sales processes and transforming them into result-driven systems. Through this dedication, developing troubleshooting technology to solve the 80/20 problem became possible all over the world. For example, what emerged was the need for Sales CPR (which is covered in our second book). Sales CPR revives sales that are "mostly dead," thereby providing a way for companies to solve their own 80/20 problem.

SELLability Technologies provides a variety of sales solutions. It's purpose is to greatly increase the number of salespeople who are prospering by increasing their ability to

SELL, thus the name, SELLability. Through SELLability, salespeople continuously improve their closing rates and all their sales abilities required to be effective throughout the sales process.

SELLability hosts the Pro Sales Network—a membership organization dedicated to helping salespeople conquer all aspects of the entire sales process. Through SELLability and the Pro Sales Network, we create an army of salespeople and organizations using SELLability technologies to greatly and positively affect the overall economy.

All of our research, development, and application are based on actual experience. We hope you find our approach to be real and applicable.

One of our key goals is to help others succeed in life and business. We are dedicated to helping you expand in your career, your business, and your life! We welcome your feedback and questions.

LET'S GET STARTED

FOREWORD

When I started out in business, I was guessing. I was young and new and having to figure it all out. To survive in the beginning, I had to be clever and study everything I could find. One of the most important parts of my business is sales. I would say on behalf of most business owners and executives I have met, business success is directly related to sales success or failure and is one of the largest sources of both happiness and stress in our lives.

Despite this fact, there were few answers that had long-term value. It seemed that the agreed upon standard was that there were only a few people that could consistently sell and you just had to find them through a numbers game of chance. There was no REAL technology for selling. Over 25 years I have seen countless so-called gurus in sales. Most of them had some good ideas, but no overall transferable technology or a duplicable process. Again, I observed a few salespeople at the top were able to gain some useful tips and increase their sales but the others were only "motivated" for a short time and then continued as inconsistent as before.

I realized that I was one of the students participating in the early stages of research and pilot testing that would eventually develop into the technology and sales process management found in this book. The origin and purpose of the research was to solve the exact problem that I was experiencing as a business owner.

I have built a business with over 1,000 trained and productive sales professionals. I consider my team true professionals with the pride and willingness to continuously improve their skills through practice and dedication to our sales process. Without a system and process, I would not have been able to sustain this growth. The first thing that was of utmost importance for me to realize was that there IS a process, or system to sales - common points to EVERY sale that happens. Knowing this is so empowering to both managers and salespeople!

The first change I made upon reading this book was re-defining the sales process as "The fundamental, systematic, repeatable, series of steps that track interactions with prospects from their first point of engagement with the salesperson, all the way through to the CLOSE." Understanding and applying this definition was the foundation of real technology for my business. The technology applied, not only created a consistently effective process, but it also transferred to my sales team and managers. This was the true value. The ability for others to learn and effectively apply the same process.

The second change I made was to shift our sales team focus away from closing. In this book, it is called re-engineering the sales process. I did find out for myself and my team that "closing was not the problem." Once I resolved the true sales problem, I doubled my existing business and had unprecedented expansion despite a pandemic and broad economic contraction.

Using the information in this book, I have continued to expand no matter what is happening with the economy. That is the big difference. Having technology that is effective for me and my entire team no matter what challenges the environment brings. Each aspect of this book is centered around getting results and improving skills. At the end of the day, only results count as it is results that pay the bills and the payroll.

For me, the book is a much-needed handbook for sales in today's current marketplace. With many insightful stories, examples, and real, usable sales questions it is a priceless tool for any organization looking to enhance the sales experience of their customers and skillset of their team. The sales professionals in our organization are confident, better prepared, and remarkably more successful because of learning and applying the technology in this book.

The world has needed an honest and insightful overhaul and upgrade of the concept of sales for a long time without a bunch of gimmicks and tricks. I know this will be a valuable tool for you and your sales team for decades to come.

Thank you, Lisa and Nick. Outstanding work!

I wish you all the success in business and life.

Michael Coleman
CEO Dynamic Expansion
Financial Services Inc.

1

RESEARCH AND DISCOVERY. THE SALES PROCESS FOUNDATION.

W e developed our sales process through years of experience and extensive research. Between us, we have over sixty years of shared experience in sales and business management. During this time, we have worked with many different industries and companies, including several of the largest in the world.

We have always been interested in what causes sales to go up, and what causes salespeople to be effective and make quotas. Why are some salespeople inconsistent, ineffective, and rarely make quotas?

Together, we decided to re-study the subjects of sales management, salespeople, sales teams, and sales programs to find out *what the world was missing.* We decided to take a fresh approach and really *look,* without bias. We wouldn't let our considerable experience get in the way of new discoveries.

We have always found that continuous improvement and learning are vital for success in life. With this mindset, we embarked on several years of research and discovery.

We refused to stop until we *found the true underlying causes for sales success and failure*—a breakthrough that was powerful enough to change every business in every industry. Discovering technology that will change an industry is rare. Finding technology that will change *all* industries is next to impossible.

A NEW TECHNOLOGY

Understanding the magnitude of our discovery, we realized that we had to share it with the world. We also knew that the technology would only be valuable if we provided it in such a way

Being a master in any subject starts with the idea
that there is always more to learn in the subject.
Once you stop learning, you stop mastering.

that others could understand it and use it to create their own success. What emerged was not only *brand-new* technology, but brand-new ways to help others learn the technology and to apply it to make their own sales teams successful.

It's worthwhile to note that when it came right down to it, all of the companies involved in our research had *the same problem.* Through the application of that research, we were able to solve it. Every time.

THE 80/20 RULE

There's a rule or law, also known as the Pareto Principle, that states that 80 percent of effects come from 20 percent of the causes. In sales, this rule is modified to state that 80 percent of sales are made by 20 percent of salespeople, which has been observed and written about over the last century.

We encountered this problem again, and again, and again. We were very effective in creating sales teams and increasing revenue and could walk into just about any company and make the sales go up. But, not every company could continue the growth and maintain it.

We knew that if we could improve the top 20 percent of salespeople, we could improve sales in a company. What if someone *wasn't* in that top 20 percent? If they were inconsistent, they were just labeled as such. There was no solution. Nobody was asking "Wait a minute. How do you fix *them?*"

We realized that in order to address this, we needed to find out what was missing. Thus began our research and discovery project.

Case Study - A $10 Million Company Revenue
(Existing Situation: Top 20% of Salespeople)

Consistently
closing sales

Top 20%

THE REALIZATION AT MICROSOFT

Our discoveries originally came about when we were doing a project with Microsoft, which was having trouble with its partner network. Both of us were experienced Microsoft Partners. Each Microsoft partner was an independently owned business, so Microsoft didn't have a direct management channel into partners—yet they needed those partners to sell their products. The 80/20 rule was very apparent in this situation. Even within the Microsoft partner network, 80 percent of the sales were being made by 20 percent of their partners.

When we went in and spoke to the partner companies, we found it there also: 80 percent of the sales were being made by 20 percent of the sales reps.

ISOLATING A NEW PATTERN: 20-60-20

In researching this further, we were able to isolate a pattern of "20 – 60 – 20." The top 20 percent were making most of the sales. The middle 60 percent wanted to sell but lacked **C**onfidence, **C**ompetence, and **C**ertainty and were inconsistent. The bottom 20 percent did not have the desire or ability to sell, and really should not have had a career in sales.

(Existing Situation: Middle 60% of Salespeople)

Ups and downs cause stress as there
is no confidence on income and sales.

Middle 60%

Inconsistent and failing
to make their quotas

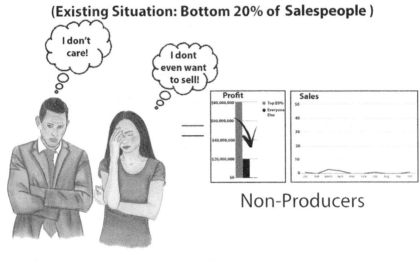

Non-Producers

Bottom 20%

The most immediate and obvious target was the middle 60 percent of the sales team. We found that if we focused on this group of salespeople, they could change an entire company.

THE IDEAL SITUATION:
Target the middle 60% & improve them!

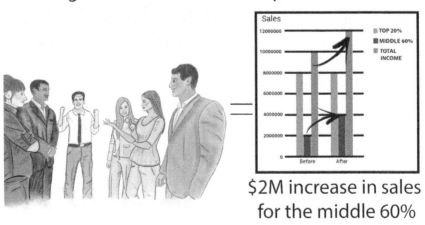

$2M increase in sales for the middle 60%

Getting the middle 60 percent to become consistent puts pressure on the top 20 percent to produce more to stay on top. So overall, the company's sales growth was transformed and maintained. Naturally, the bottom 20 percent were replaced or were just no longer needed.

THE IDEAL SITUATION:

Target the middle 60% & improve them, thereby putting pressure on the top 20% to do even better.

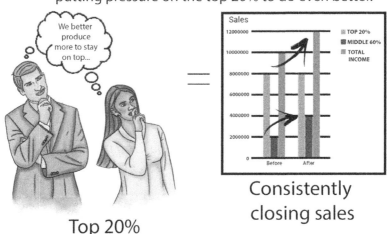

Top 20%

Consistently closing sales

OVER-FOCUS ON CLOSING

When we began digging in to resolve these problems, we realized that despite billions of dollars being spent yearly on sales training, the 80/20 rule persisted—going all the way back to the 1940s when it was observed. It had *never* been resolved.

One of the major discoveries we made was that most sales training focuses almost exclusively on closing. Of course, closing is important as that's where the money is made. But, there's a great deal more to a sales process than closing.

You see this all around. Just go into a mall; start walking into stores and meeting salespeople. You'll find that every conversation begins with a push toward the close. Even "Can I help you?" is an assumption that you need help, rather than a simple welcome to the store.

What emerged was a simple, observable fact: If all of that money and time was being spent on improving sales, but 80/20 was still a problem, and the focus of that money and time was on closing, then **closing must not be the problem!**

CLOSING WAS PART OF THE PROBLEM

In fact, we found that the focus on closing in sales training programs was actually in part *causing the problem!*

When it came down to it, this was the number one reason salespeople have had so much trouble, and such bad reputations, down through the years: from the very beginning of the conversation, they're trying to *close the prospect.*

Trying to close as the main focus of sales training, along with the overall generational decline in communication skills has created a recipe for sales program failure. It has also made 80/20 an even more solid reality.

THE FOCUS ON CLOSING, A FAILED SOLUTION TO INCREASE SALES, WENT UNNOTICED AND BECOME THE STANDARD

In actuality, attempting to skip right to the close is a poor solution to the problem of not knowing and applying the vital

steps of the sales process. If you want a live demonstration of how ineffective such a thing is, just walk up to someone and try to close them on a sale. You can feel that resistance.

LOST COMMUNICATION SKILLS, THE ROOT OF THE PROBLEM

This overemphasis on closing comes from the fact that the earlier sales process steps rely on being an expert in communication, which unfortunately, is a missing ability (SELL ability) in sales today. As technology and social media have taken over, communication skills have radically declined. By using social media, people can avoid live communication. This has resulted in a lack of trust between people.

There have been many poor solutions created to solve this lack of communication expertise. Unfortunately, none have been effective and have made the 80/20 rule even more solid. If you cannot effectively communicate, you skip the sales process steps and just try to close your prospects.

AVOIDING THE CLOSER AT THE CAR DEALER

A prime example exists in the auto industry, famous for the car salesman just trying to "make a deal." Such practices made the public resist going to the dealer. Automaker Saturn attempted to solve this resistance by creating a button you could pin on your shirt while you were on their car lot that said: "Just Looking." This was supposed to "protect you" from their salespeople who were just trying to close you.

The next poor solution put into practice was to put a layer between the initial salesperson and the "closer." This resulted in the initial salesperson being less skilled and not having all the details, which caused them to have to defer to the person in finance who really had the information.

The only job of the initial salesperson was to get you excited enough to sit down with the sales manager or finance manager who then crushed you into what could turn out to be a good *or* bad deal—you basically had a 50-50 shot. This, of course, created further public resistance to the sales process.

CUSTOMER SERVICE - A LOST ART IN SALES

In the 1990s, did you notice that we received less and less service from the big department stores? The public had been complaining about salespeople being too high-pressure so some genius came up with the unusual solution of taking sales commissions away from salespeople instead of simply fixing their communication skills. The result, of course, was de-motivated salespeople who no longer cared about servicing the customer.

What the executives in these stores forgot was that a prime key to their success was *great customer service!* People come into your store for a reason: they have interest! If they are well taken care of, they will often buy more than they came for. But if salespeople don't care they will not take great care of the customer. Customers *will buy less.*

Customer service is key and includes (as we'll cover in detail later) manners and granting importance. These are factors that have become lost to the detriment of customers, salespeople, business owners, and the overall economy.

A fantastic example of the importance of service in sales is in the movie *Pretty Woman.* Remember the sequence in which Julia Roberts' character is shopping on Rodeo Drive, and an extremely snobbish salesperson refuses to service her, thinking she could never afford the prices?

After the hero of the film, Edward, takes her to another store and sets her up with great service, she buys practically the entire store. She goes back to the original store, wearing some of the clothes she bought and informs the arrogant salesperson who wouldn't service her that she had made a "big mistake. Huge."

SALES RESISTANCE FROM YOUR PROSPECT

We could all agree that the most basic problem for sales-people, the one that salespeople work hardest to overcome, is that prospects naturally resist being "sold" a product or service. Sales Professionalism could be summed up as having the **abilities** to overcome sales resistance and guide the prospect to the product or service solution that ultimately exceeds their expectations.

Why do prospects resist salespeople (and we all do it)? Well, how many of us have had at least one bad experience with a salesperson? Most of us have had many bad experiences with salespeople and the buying process. Think about it: if 80 percent of sales are done by 20 percent of salespeople, it makes sense that 8 out of 10 salespeople or 8 out of 10 buying processes are going to be bad. This is where the resistance comes from. We expect the process to be painful; so, we resist.

The problem for salespeople is that we *don't like* resistance. We resist the prospect's resistance, resulting in prospects resisting salespeople and salespeople resisting the prospect's resistance. What a strange way to buy products and services! Unfortunately, it is the reality.

The over-focus on closing causes salespeople to focus on closing from the time they greet the prospect. In our research, we found this to be the number one reason for low closing rates. As we'll see in the Sales Process chapter, closing is the *end* of the sales process. Closing by itself is not going to overcome sales resistance.

SALES RESISTANCE MUST BE HANDLED PRIOR TO THE CLOSE

By the time the close happens, sales resistance better have been overcome already, or the close just won't occur. Sales resistance must be dealt with somewhere in the sales process *prior* to the close.

The skills used to overcome sales resistance are all too often not learned at all or learned badly. As buyers, most of us can recall bad experiences we've had with salespeople who obviously never learned these skills.

When we think of sales, we tend to associate it with dishonesty and betrayal. We do not want to be "sold" something. Stories circulate of people being tricked by salespeople and ending up with bad products or poor service.

People, of course, don't want such problems, and then comes a general resistance to salespeople, and the overall opinion that sales is a bad career. The truth is, sales is the only job every business in the world must have. If you are a great salesperson, it's a great career and you will always have a job.

DECLINE IN SELLING SKILLS AND THE MOVE ONLINE

In the last decade, major retailers have been going online—no doubt led by the success of Amazon. However, there is another reason for this move that isn't being seen.

The truth is, people do best with people. A high percentage of buyers would still rather go in person to see a product and be educated about it, perhaps even after researching it online. But problems arise when they go in, meet a salesperson, and the salesperson is clumsy and unskilled at selling. As we've covered, 8 out of 10 salespeople you meet are going to handle you poorly. In the end you're driven to, "Okay. I'll just go online."

Or, worse, you never buy the product or service. We have taken to asking in our sales workshops, "How many of you are considering buying something?" Interestingly, *everyone in the room* was thinking about making some major purchase. They had done their homework and had been thinking about this purchase for 3 months, 6 months, a year, or longer.

We could (and did) take any one of those people, with the product that they had been thinking about, and sell that product to them right then and there, using a full, professional, standard sales process.

We did the job that some poor salesperson failed to do at some time in the past. If we'd been paid the commissions from these sales, we probably could have retired by now!

SALES ABILITIES ARE FOR PEOPLE, NOT AUTOMATION

What is the problem these companies are trying to solve by making the move online? They're trying to solve, through automation, the fact that sales, customer service, and communication **abilities** have been declining for years.

If you go back 20 or 30 years, such **abilities** were possessed by all the top salespeople—they serviced, had great communication skills, and built relationships. Honestly, companies are losing money because of the move online.

Salespeople with great communication skills, having built relationships, will make more sales than an online service ever could. A salesperson who develops the relationship, and who delivers great service to the customer, is going to sell a lot more products. Instead, we do a high volume of sales online, but the average sale is less.

The other unintended consequence is product returns. The percentage of returns from online shopping has created more business for the shipping companies and created a whole new world of poor solutions and policies. The returns have become such an expensive consequence that some companies have added their own shipping division to reduce the cost of handling returns.

Overall, we are solving the wrong problem. All of us would love some great customer service!

Lost Opportunity And Lost Income

Great Customer Service = Higher Average Sale

SHIFT OF FOCUS FROM CLOSING
TO CUSTOMER SERVICE

Most salespeople have forgotten—or perhaps they were never taught—that CLOSING is all about SERVICE. If you look at the good experiences you might have had with sales, you'll realize those salespeople truly served you. Salespeople who are ignorant of this fact rarely make that close and end up mostly annoying people.

The move towards online sales made the need for great customer service even more important. Taking care of someone online or over the phone requires an even higher level of customer service skill. This skill will become even more valuable as the future moves more and more to a virtual sales process.

We found that shifting the focus of sales teams from closing to customer service went a long way to solving the 80/20 issues, especially among the middle 60 percent of salespeople.

You should approach a prospect as if they are going to be a customer for life. Work on developing a level of trust both ways. Doing so takes the focus off closing and places it on customer service. Making this one change can double the closing rate of a sales team.

SPECIAL NOTE ON "JUST-LOOKING"

Many customers, especially in a retail environment, will put off a salesperson by saying they're just looking. Your prospect is generally way too busy to be just looking.

According to a recent article in the *New York Times*[1], the average American is shown over 5,000 messages *per day* through push marketing (radio, TV, social media, email, text, billboards and others). This comes out to over 35,000 messages per week, and over 150,000 messages per month.

Think about it: if a prospect reaches out to *you* after potentially receiving tens of thousands of offers, the first thing you should do is *welcome them, thank them so much for thinking of you, and provide them with amazing customer service from the moment they reach out!*

Remember, from the sea of possibilities your prospect could spend time on, they chose you! The first steps are to welcome them with good manners and grant them importance, especially for taking the time to reach out to you.

Just this one focus may bring a percentage of those customers who might otherwise go elsewhere right back

---

[1] https://www.nytimes.com/2007/01/15/business/media/15everywhere.html

to see you because most customers do want great customer service and personal attention. If you can provide it, you have a definite advantage in today's market because most people have been driven elsewhere due to *poor* customer service.

As you can see, customers are not really "just looking." Customers react to poor customer service by pretending they are just looking.

Irresistible and Trustable!

Resistible and Untrustworthy!

DOES SALES AS A NUMBERS GAME REALLY WORK?

There's another statistic you should know about and bear in mind. On average, 20 percent of your prospects, or 2 out of 10, will buy your product or service anyway. They have already decided before they reached out to your company. Many companies and salespeople know about this statistic and survive on that 20 percent closing rate.

This contributes to the 80/20 rule and is one of the reasons the middle 60% will sometimes sell inconsistently. This creates false hope for the salesperson and management. It also leads to what is commonly known as "sales is a numbers game."

Here's a quick case study on this numbers game:

- If your product or service sells for $1,000.00, then 10 prospects at a 20 percent closing rate = $2,000.00
- Using the theory of this numbers game, let's double your money: 20 prospects at a 20 percent closing rate = $4,000.00
- Using the theory of this numbers game, let's *triple* your money: 30 prospects at a 20 percent closing rate = $6,000.00

Note: At this point, you likely max out your ability to handle the number of prospects required for the numbers game!

THIS 20 PERCENT CLOSING RATE IS HIGHLY UNPROFITABLE

A company expends an incredible amount of marketing time and money to get those 10 prospects, to close 2. All

Numbers game with a 20% closing rate

the time and money spent to obtain the other 8 prospects is wasted. Closing 4 out of 10 prospects, or a 40 percent closing rate, is where profitability starts. The real profit begins as the closing rate goes higher. Salespeople need to generate a 40 percent closing rate just to cover their own costs.

Now let's look at this numbers game using SELLability Technology, which would give you **at least** a 40 percent closing rate:

10 prospects at a 40 percent closing rate = $4,000.00.

20 prospects at a 40 percent closing rate = $8,000.00

30 prospects at a 40 percent closing rate = $12,000.00

Note: At this point, you still max out your ability to handle the number of prospects—but you end up with $12,000.00 instead of $6,000.00

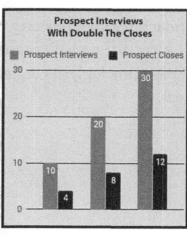

Continuous Improvement, Double Your Closing Rate To 40%.

Prospect Interviews With Double The Closes

Prospect Interviews | Prospect Closes

This all may seem obvious, but if that were true, why all the focus on the numbers game? If everybody knew, 80/20 would have been solved long ago. But 80/20 still dominates after more than 70 years of sales training and sales solutions! It is time for a brand-new technology with new solutions.

BEING THE IRRESISTIBLE, CARING SALESPERSON

We've touched on remembering times when you've been handled badly by a salesperson. Now, instead, recall a time when a salesperson did a great job caring for you and serving you. Following that sale, your viewpoint of salespeople might have changed for the better, but only concerning that one experience. If we could bring *every* salesperson up to the point of creating that kind of result, we could change society's overall opinion of salespeople.

The irresistible salesperson guides a prospect skillfully through the sales process.

Now that we have covered the research and development of the technology, let's begin with the basics: The Sales Process itself.

2

THE SALES PROCESS

EACH SALES PROCESS STEP MUST HAVE A VERIFIABLE RESULT

Through our research and our experience, we have discovered that closing was never a salesperson's problem. In fact, the persistent problem is the *lack of a reliable, accurate, and result-driven sales process followed step by step.* If such a process isn't learned, followed, and verified step by step, the close doesn't happen.

This is a pretty simple process. The key difference is that each step has an exact result, which is verifiable. You may have more detail in your particular sales process, which is fine, but you'll find this process encompasses any sales process out there. The point is, having a result based-sales process, and thoroughly learning and drilling it, is completely vital to sales success.

We created this sales process with a great deal of consideration, research, and testing. In fact, we piloted, tested, and used it ourselves, in our own companies and in other companies, refining it the entire way before publishing it broadly.

During the pilot phase of the sales process development, one company with a 600+ sales force was getting inconsistent results. After much analysis, troubleshooting, and time, we found that the salespeople were not consistently using the sales process. In every case where there were mixed results, it was discovered the salesperson did not follow the full sales process nor did they understand the importance of each step being a verified result.

Furthermore, when they went back and filled in the missing steps in that sales process, the deal closed. Moral of this story: ensure your entire sales force consistently practices the sales process through role-play drills! Each salesperson needs to know and follow every step of your sales process to its fullest to ensure the deal closes when the time comes. This is the difference between the top 20% of salespeople and the other 80% who are inconsistent or not effective at all.

MOTIVATION IS TIED TO SALES PROCESS RESULTS

In most books and articles about selling, experts discuss the importance of sales mindset and motivation. One of the many different tactics we use in SELLability is that *motivation is tied to results at each step of the sales process.*

We tie motivation to results with the sales process. With the sales process, results are ensured every step of the way, as each step of the sales process has its own result that must be achieved before moving on to the next step.

Motivation will only last if you're getting results. Each completed step of the sales process is a result that will keep the salesperson motivated. Without consistent results being achieved, motivation fades away. The top 20% of salespeople know the steps and verify results at each step of the sales process.

WORKING THE SALES PROCESS BACKWARD

First, we will work the sales process backward, as that's how it was researched. It was literally reverse-engineered from the close. We researched and worked with thousands of salespeople, sales managers, and business owners engineering the process step by step, backward from the close.

This was an intensive, highly detailed process. We kept asking "what happens just prior?" We persisted until a consistently effective, step-by-step process was revealed across every industry we researched. We will take you along the path we walked during our research. Note each step has an exact result.

CLOSING

At the end comes closing. It's the last step of the process. This includes completing all the paperwork contracts and logistics necessary to successfully transition the prospect to an actual customer and smoothly start the delivery process.

Transitioning the customer to your delivery team with all details is critical in order for the delivery to exceed the expectations you have communicated during the sales process.

In this way, you are guaranteed further sales and referrals from this customer, which is vital to your ongoing success.

It can happen that delivery doesn't go well, or has problems. The customer keeps bouncing back to the salesperson because the salesperson is who the customer was in the best communication with. This problem has a high chance of being solved by completing this final step, the transition of the customer to the delivery team, with both the salesperson and a representative of the delivery team present.

This needs to be done to create total agreement on what will occur during delivery between the salesperson, the customer, and the delivery representative. The delivery person in charge of that customer's account should emphasize that if there's a problem, the prospect should call them. This establishes the customer's relationship with the delivery team.

A few years ago, a large Microsoft partner contacted SELL-ability because they had encountered a downtrend in their revenue. They were also experiencing order cancellations and customer issues in record numbers. To top it off, their sales and delivery departments were at each other's throats.

When we got to the bottom of it, we found the Customer Sale form the sales teams had been using was missing critical information. If that information had been there and the transition had occurred as described above, it would have helped the delivery team to ensure each customer received exactly what they had ordered, with any and all instructions carried out as requested. Happy customers = happy salespeople = more sales.

Moral of this story: the transition from the sales team to the delivery team is critical, adding up to customer satisfaction and thus, future orders and referrals.

The end result here is that the delivery person in charge of the customer's account takes full responsibility for the customer and the customer's service. In this way, the customer, if they have an issue, will maintain their communication with that person. If you fail to have someone in your delivery team fully responsible for that customer account, it will always come back to the salesperson and this will stop your sales.

Closing Result: The successful transition of the prospect from the salesperson to the delivery team. This includes all the final logistics and paperwork required to finalize the sale. This frees up the salesperson to completely focus on the sales process with another customer. Attention is no longer tied up in the worry of whether or not the previous customer will be taken care of.

CLOSED- Successful transition to delivery!

The result of the closing step is the successful transition of the prospect from the salesperson to the delivery team. This frees up the salesperson to completely focus on the sales process with another customer. Attention is no longer tied up in the worry of whether or not the previous customer will be taken care of.

AGREEMENT: WHAT HAPPENS BEFORE THE CLOSING STEP?

Just before closing is the Agreement step. You have brought the prospect all the way through the sales process. You've

Agreement Result:
During or at the end of the Agreement step, the customer has firmly decided to buy and has voiced that decision.

actually, or virtually, shaken hands and the prospect has decided to purchase. At this point, the prospect or customer has decided to buy. It is at this step that you will get the last of the objections, and where you will need to deal with them. Ideally, of course, the objections have been handled in the previous steps.

There's a small step in between Agreement and Closing where you handle paperwork, logistics, and anything else you need to wrap up and that takes you from Agreement to Close.

We were once called into a company as they had a multi-million dollar deal that had been stalled for several months. They had tried everything to get it moving again and were about to give up on it despite it being so close to closing. Ironically, in their Sales CPR Clinic[1], they found the deal itself was solid.

The problem was that *the salesperson did not complete all actions within the Agreement section of the sales process.* There was one objection that had come up towards the end of the Agreement section, and a few logistics that needed to be taken care of. All of this was easily handled and the deal successfully closed within 8 days of their Sales CPR Clinic.

Agreement result: During, or at the end of, the Agreement step, the customer has firmly decided to buy and has voiced that decision.

---

[1] A service SELLability provides to revive dead sales.

Agreement result: During or at the end of the Agreement step, the customer has firmly decided to buy and has voiced that decision.

EDUCATION: WHAT HAPPENS JUST BEFORE THE AGREEMENT STEP?

Prior to Agreement is the Education step. Education is incredibly important. Your prospect must totally understand *why* your product or service is essential to *their* lives or *their* business. These five factors must be part of the Education step:

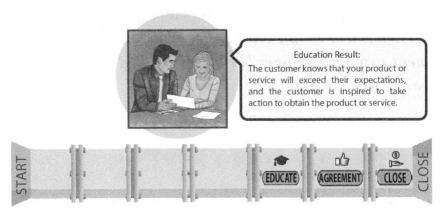

1. Saving the prospect time
2. Saving the prospect money
3. Making the prospect money
4. Solving the prospect's problems
5. Helping them achieve their goals

How you address these 5 factors is vitally important. One of the top complaints about salespeople, by survey, is that they talk too much and the place where they talk too much is right here on the Education step.

The Education step follows the Qualify step (which you will read about next). The Education step is a laser-precise process that educates the prospect based *exactly* on the customer complaints or needs and wants discovered in the Qualify step.

Note that even though you are selling the same product or service to every prospect, each Education step will be unique and different, as it is based on that particular prospect's experience, needs and wants.

One of our breakthrough discoveries in researching the sales process was that *Education only supports exactly what information you've obtained earlier from the prospect's viewpoint, in the Qualify step of the process.*

We found that salespeople who overeducated, in other words, attempted to educate the prospect on anything and everything about the product or service, whether it had anything to do with the prospect's problems or not, lost the prospect's interest.

The prospect will only remain interested to the degree that you precisely educate them about *their* problems, needs, and wants, addressing the five factors listed above.

At one point, we were doing an endless amount of testing on the sales process. We were working with a large company that had agreed to test our SELLability sales process and technology, starting with their least productive sales team. That team went on to become one of the most productive teams the company had ever experienced.

The missing key element was their ability to customize the presentation for each individual sale based on the knowledge, experiences, and emotions of each individual prospect. The education process is not a rote process. It is not something to be repeated verbatim, step by step, but more like a tailor-made educational process *custom-made* for each prospect based on their individual needs. Once we were able to get the sales team to understand this principle, the sales came pouring in.

This wasn't an overnight accomplishment. It required a lot of role-play drilling to improve each of the sales team members' ability to think on their feet, using the standard education steps but customizing as they went.

Moral of the story: the Education step is one of the most important steps of the sales process. The Education step is not a rote activity. While the Education step itself has a set standard and set steps towards bringing a prospect to a full conceptual understanding of your product or service, not every prospect needs to be educated in the exact same way, or to the same extent, on each step.

The Education step should be individualized to specifically address each particular prospect and their needs and wants. If you do this, you will be very successful.

At the end of the Education step, your prospect should be inspired to take action. When you've educated someone and properly inspired them, based on their goals, their dreams, their interests, their problems, how do you think you'll do in closing the sale? Answer: brilliantly.

Many salespeople skip straight to the Close. Many other salespeople skip straight to this Education step without going through any of the steps prior. We've all experienced this. When it happens, the prospect is immediately bored because, prior to launching into a long-winded explanation of their product or service, the salesperson hasn't discovered anything about the prospect: their needs, wants, desires, or problems. There's no alignment of the Education to something the prospect might actually be interested in.

In either scenario, skipping to Education or skipping to the Close, you'll never inspire anyone into action; so, you'll never get to Agreement, and then to the actual Close. This is why 80 percent of salespeople fail to close.

Education result: The customer knows that your product or service will exceed their expectations, and the customer is inspired to take action to obtain the product or service.

Education result: The customer knows that your product or service will exceed their expectations, and the customer is inspired to take action to obtain the product or service.

QUALIFYING: WHAT MUST HAPPEN JUST BEFORE EDUCATION?

Qualifying is the step prior to Education. Here, you're finding out why the prospect should purchase your product or service, from *their* point of view; *not* from the salesperson's point of view! The result of the first step, Contact and Interview, is trust and it is critical here. At this point, the prospect trusts you enough to tell you what they truly think, which is what you're going to find out in this step. The key to this is asking questions that cause your prospects to take a look for themselves. You must truly be interested in them and their answers. Here are a few example questions:

- What inspired them to contact you in the first place?
- What issues are they running into that caused them to call?

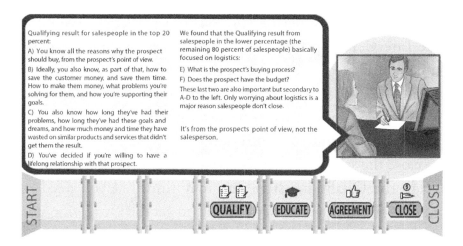

Qualifying result for salespeople in the top 20 percent:

A) You know all the reasons why the prospect should buy, from the prospect's point of view.

B) Ideally, you also know, as part of that, how to save the customer money, and save them time. How to make them money, what problems you're solving for them, and how you're supporting their goals.

C) You also know how long they've had their problems, how long they've had these goals and dreams, and how much money and time they have wasted on similar products and services that didn't get them the result.

D) You've decided if you're willing to have a lifelong relationship with that prospect.

We found that the Qualifying result from salespeople in the lower percentage (the remaining 80 percent of salespeople) basically focused on logistics:

E) What is the prospect's buying process?

F) Does the prospect have the budget?

These last two are also important but secondary to A-D to the left. Only worrying about logistics is a major reason salespeople don't close.

It's from the prospects point of view, not the salesperson.

START | QUALIFY | EDUCATE | AGREEMENT | CLOSE

- How long have they had those issues, or how long have they been thinking about this purchase?
- What are their goals and dreams, and how long have they had them?
- What problems are they having with their existing product or service?
- How are those problems affecting their quality of life?
- If they didn't have those problems, how would their life change?

The answers to these questions are very important later on in the sales process.

If you have built trust by granting importance in previous steps (more on that later), the prospect will feel comfortable providing true answers to these questions. You must arrive at this step with the prospect trusting you enough to tell you what they truly think in relation to their needs, wants, and problems.

The trap a salesperson can fall into is that they've done the Interview step (explained in the next section) so many times that they go into a meeting assuming they already know what issues the prospect has and why they should purchase. This completely robs a prospect of their own conviction and determination and you won't develop the trust vitally needed to close the sale.

In the Qualifying step, you may find that you need to educate the prospect somewhat, just to get the Qualifying step done. But, mainly you're just trying to find out all about the prospect's point of view in relation to what you're offering.

Qualifying result for salespeople in the top 20 percent:
- *a) You know all the reasons the prospect should buy, from the prospect's point of view.*
- *b) Ideally, you also know, as part of that, how to save the customer money and time; how to make them money; what problems you're solving for them; and how you're supporting their goals.*
- *c) You also know how long they've had their problems, how long they've had those goals and dreams, and how much money and time they have wasted on similar products and services that didn't get them their result.*
- *d) You've decided if you're willing to have a lifelong relationship with that prospect.*
- *e) You know the prospect's buying process.*
- *f) You know the prospect has the budget.*

Qualifying result from salespeople in the lower 80 percent basically focused on logistics (e and f above):

e) What is the prospect's buying process?

f) Does the prospect have the budget?

These last two are also important but secondary to a - d.
Only worrying about logistics is a major reason salespeople
don't close.

Qualifying Result

Qualifying result for salespeople
in the top 20 percent:

a) You know all the reasons why the prospect
   should buy, from the prospect's point of view.

b) Ideally, you also know, as part of that,
   how to save the customer money,
   and save them time. How to make them
   money, what problems you're solving for
   them, and how you're supporting their goals.

c) You also know how long they've had their
   problems, how long they've had those goals
   and dreams, and how much money and time
   have they wasted on similar products and
   services that didn't get them the result.

d) You've decided if you're willing to have a
   lifelong relationship with that prospect.

Qualifying Focused on Logistics

We found that the
Qualifying result from
salespeople in the lower percentage
(the remaining 80 percent of salespeople)
basically focused on logistics:

• What is the prospect's buying process?

• Does the prospect have the budget?

These 2 points are important,
but secondary. Only worrying about
logistics is a major reason salespeople
don't close.

SCARCITY NOTE

Following this process exactly, you'll find about 20 percent, or 2 out of 10, are *not* qualified. But, letting 2 out of 10 go would be no big deal, as long as you have enough prospects.

Scarcity of prospects causes you to hold onto unqualified prospects.

How many of you have been in the situation where you knew you shouldn't make that sale because the person was unqualified, but you were trying to make a quota or you needed the money, so you went ahead and closed it anyway? You then found, 2 weeks later, you would pay good money to get rid of that customer. You knew, during that sales process, that you shouldn't close them.

We once had a long-term customer that required a lot of special attention, so much in fact, that we had to assign the Vice President of Sales as his only contact. He was given quite a few discounts and required a lot of extra care and attention just to keep him as a customer. This resulted in having to make allowances and special changes along the entire customer service and delivery line just for him. In all, an extra 10 hours were spent on each order the company received from him in comparison with every other customer.

In truth, this customer wasn't qualified for the products and by ignoring this fact we wasted an enormous amount of time and money. In the end, we were able to move this customer on to another service in a different company that he was more qualified for.

The result? We received an influx of qualified customers that we now had room to service and experienced an increase in sustained revenue.

Moral of the story: Only close qualified leads AND never have a scarcity of prospects flowing into your sales process.

CONTACT AND INTERVIEW: WHAT RESULT MUST YOU HAVE TO SUCCESSFULLY QUALIFY YOUR PROSPECT?

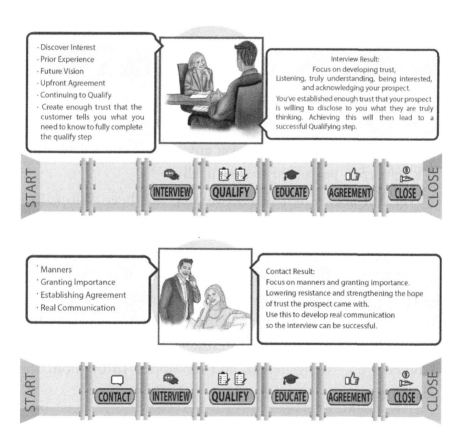

Before Qualifying comes Contact and Interview, a very important step in the sales process. One of the key reasons we found behind the 80/20 problem is that salespeople fail at this step. What they fail to do is to establish enough trust with the prospect that they are willing to tell the salesperson what they are truly thinking. You won't make it through the Qualifying step if you haven't done the Contact and Interview steps correctly and completely. That's because, in order to get a prospect to tell you about their lives, their hopes, their dreams, and their problems, they need to trust you enough to tell you what they're really thinking.

It is during this stage that you create trust with the prospect. Symptoms of not having developed enough trust are:

- the prospect didn't call you back
- the prospect didn't email you back
- the prospect doesn't answer any kind of communication either in person or electronically

We can always tell when this step has been skipped or skimped on because there's the evidence, every time: no communication back.

Remember, through all the thousands of messages they had prior to calling you, they had an interest in your product or service. They wouldn't have reached out to you unless they were interested. That interest is fragile, so it must be handled well, strengthened, and developed throughout the sales process.

ESTABLISHING TRUST: VITAL TO CREATE AND STRENGTHEN THROUGHOUT EVERY STEP OF THE SALES PROCESS.

If the buying process was rational and logical, as most sales training says it is, we wouldn't need salespeople, would we? We'd just need people to take orders. But in fact, the buying process is reactive and emotional, and for the buyer to actually view a product or service rationally and make a correct decision, the salesperson needs to establish *trust* with that buyer. Trust breaks down the sales resistance of the prospect, and allows them to logically look at your product or service.

Establishing trust is the first job of the salesperson, which is why it comes under the *Contact and Interview* step of the sales process.

How does the establishment of trust come about? By breaking through the barrier between *social* and *real* communication.

When you arrive at work in the morning, and you ask how people are, how do they nearly always answer? "Fine." Are they? Maybe so, maybe not. But it's just a social answer, isn't it?

A person has been going through life pretending everything is "fine" simply because they've never (or rarely) come across anyone they can trust enough to stop pretending. They need a real, caring person to listen, understand, and guide them to a real solution.

Because of previous bad sales experiences and lack of trust, people tend to resist salespeople. As part of this resistance, they tend to act as if everything is fine. They're not telling you everything they're thinking until you start to develop trust, until they start to *develop hope* that they can trust you. At that point it's fragile, so you need to continue to develop that trust, causing the prospect to develop more and more hope, up to the point where they realize that it's real and they can truly trust you.

In sales, right from the very beginning, you must establish enough trust that your prospect is willing to disclose to you what they really think. At the beginning, when you first begin to develop trust, you're actually developing hope. You need to have a real conversation, not a social one. The reason most sales processes don't end up in a sale is simply that by the time we get to the close, we're still having a social conversation.

At the point where trust actually occurs, you can transition and have a very successful Qualifying process. There can be

Contact Result
Focus on Manners & Granting Importance
"Lowering Resistance - Hope of Trust"

Contact and Interview result: You've established enough trust that your prospect is willing to disclose to you what they are truly thinking.
Achieving this will then lead to a successful Qualifying step.

Contact and Interview result: You've established enough trust that your prospect is willing to disclose to you what they are truly thinking. Achieving this will then lead to a successful Qualifying step.

overlap between the two, but what you're going for is true trust. It has to develop from hope to real trust.

This requires real communication skills which, as we'll cover later, are *not* improved through digital devices. Each of us has the ability to communicate. To master communication, we must continuously improve communication skills.

Research Result:
You've cared enough to establish a foundation of information which is going to allow the Contact and Interview step to go more smoothly. This is going to allow you to develop trust much more efficiently.

Contact and Interview result: You've established REAL communication and developed enough trust that your prospect is willing to disclose to you what they are truly thinking. Achieving this will lead to a successful Qualifying step.

A foundation of trust will lead you all the way through the sales process and you'll need to strengthen it as you go.

RESEARCH: WHAT SHOULD HAPPEN BEFORE CONTACT AND INTERVIEW TO EFFECTIVELY OPEN COMMUNICATION AND BUILD TRUST?

There is a step prior to making the initial contact, and that is Research. A massive mistake salespeople make is not researching their prospects. Do your homework! Really understand your prospect before you meet them. Do they know the same people you know? Today, with social media, this step is much easier than it was years back. For example, you can discover you have a friend in common; call that friend and gain an introduction. Research can and should be done throughout the entire sales process.

Here are some examples of basic points of Research:

- Research your prospect on the internet, LinkedIn, and your prospect's company website to find biographical and career information, so you can get familiar with the prospect.
- Research your prospect's company using their website and the internet.
- Research the company's products or services to become familiar with them and how they could fit with the

products or services you are selling. See how they describe their products and services—high quality, great value, discount price, and so on.

- Research common connections including vendors, mutual friends, and colleagues. Use these connections to develop a better understanding of your prospect's likes, dislikes, and interests.

- Check your CRM (Customer Relationship Management software). It seems obvious, but your company's own CRM information can be a valuable tool and give good insight towards learning more about your prospects. Even researching previous engagements can provide good insight into what did or didn't work previously.

- Other Social Media: Facebook, Instagram, Twitter, can all be valuable platforms to gain information on your prospect.

- Industry News: Check to see what is out there on the internet. Recent news articles provide an excellent way to define discussion structure around relevant topics important to the prospect.

- Their company's blog.

- Their competitors' websites, press releases, and messaging.

- Their Google results.

- Personnel recruiting sites – you can at least gain insight into the company's culture, not to mention being able to see what areas the company is currently investing in (the areas where the company is currently hiring shows where they are investing).

- Internet platforms like Crunchbase – This platform has a lot of valuable information, including a way to discover your prospect's acquisition history, timeline, news, competitors, former employees, customers and partners, and even board members and advisors, and more.

Note: If you are unable to research your prospects before you meet them, you can use the above as a guide for questions to ask during the Contact and Interview step. Also, asking these questions to every customer is a form of research. You will find similarities and differences you can use as research to help you with future prospects.

Research result: You've cared enough to establish a foundation of information that is going to allow the Contact and Interview step to go more smoothly. This is going to allow you to develop trust much more efficiently.

Research result: You've cared enough to established a foundation of information which is going to allow the Contact and Interview step to go more smoothly. This is going to allow you to develop trust much more efficiently.

You could actually say that research is being done so you don't have to cold-call. There's enough research available online and from your referral base that there is no longer a need for cold calls.

The more information you have on the person you're calling before you actually make the call, the more tailored you can slant your conversation towards their likes and dislikes. After all, the reason people pick up the phone for friends is that they have something in common, a shared reality on one or more subjects.

Making a cold call can be uncomfortable, but if you take the time to learn some information that will be known and possibly liked and admired by your prospect, you will have the advantage you need to get yourself in the door and even keep the conversation going long enough to create a relationship you can use.

Failure to analyze strengths and weaknesses during the sales process is a sales killer. We found most salespeople are so relieved and happy after a close that they never go back and review why the sale closed. After a sale closes, go back and review what you learned and what you would change or improve. This is all part of the SELLability continuous improvement system.

PROSPECTING: WHAT MUST HAPPEN IN ABUNDANCE BEFORE THE RESEARCH STEP TO PREVENT SCARCITY?

Prospecting is the step prior to Research. Prospecting consists of four parts, equally important.

PROSPECTS

Abundance of qualified prospects
responding to your marketing
campaign and reaching for your
products and services.

a) Define your public, meaning know all about the people you are trying to sell to. This means factors such as position in a company, age, gender (if applicable), marital status, and any other qualification which brings them closer to being an ideal prospect for your product or service.

It just doesn't make sense to try to target everyone. It takes time, energy, and money, which will produce better results if invested in a target audience. Define your target market. Find out what they like and dislike. There are four types of people who fit into your brand's target audience:

- The person who will pay you
- The person who influences the person who pays you
- The person who supports you
- The person who will use the product or service

All four of these are important and you must account for each one.

b) Survey your public to understand how they think. Find out their needs, wants, hopes, and dreams. You need to truly know these people.

c) Know your product or service, what makes you different (your Unique Selling Proposition, or USP), and have a fast, powerful "elevator pitch" to quickly give someone. Once you have it, practice it on different people. Revise it until you have a very easy, fast, and simple way to make your product or service understood by others.

The key to prospecting is being interested in and understanding your target market and having total confidence in introducing them to what you do.

d) Develop and provide valuable free content based on everything you learn in the three steps above (a-c). This starts a communication and trust with your prospects before you ever meet them.

Prospecting result: You've developed a huge database of potential prospects, of the target public that will buy your products or services. You have provided that public with valuable free content, keeping them actively in communication with your company, resulting in your company being considered a valuable source of information and a company the prospects can TRUST! With that in place, you can now market to those prospects causing them to reach for your products and services. You can then research and develop them into prospects who will smoothly go into communication at the Contact step and move through your sales process.

A trusted source of information.

You've developed a huge database of potential prospects that will buy your products and provided them with valuable free content. This keeps them in active communication with your company resulting in your company being considered a valuable source of information and a company they can TRUST! You can now research and then contact them developing them into prospects who will smoothly go into communication at the contact step of the sales process.

THE SALES PROCESS IN SEQUENCE

As you can see, we reverse-engineered the sales process steps, transforming them into a result-driven system, which is key to resolving the 80/20 problem. Now let's look at the sales process in sequence.

Prospecting— You've developed a huge database of potential prospects, of the public who will buy your products or services. You have provided them with valuable free content, keeping them actively in communication with your company, resulting in your company being considered a valuable source of information *and* a company the prospects can *trust*!

With that in place, you can now market to those prospects causing them to reach for your products and services. You can then research and develop them into prospects who will smoothly go into communication at the Contact step and move through your sales process.

Research—You've cared enough to establish a foundation of information that is going to allow the Contact and Interview step to go more smoothly. This is going to allow you to develop trust much more efficiently.

Contact and Interview—You've established *real* communication and developed enough trust that your prospect is willing to disclose to you what they are truly thinking. Achieving this will then lead to a successful Qualifying step.

Qualifying—

a) You know all the reasons the prospect should buy, from the prospect's point of view.

b) Ideally, you also know, as part of that, how to save the customer money, and save them time. How to make them money, what problems you're solving for them, and how you're supporting their goals.

c) You now know how long they've had their problems, how long they've had those goals and dreams, and how much money and time they have wasted on similar products and services that didn't get them the result.

d) You've decided if you're willing to have a lifelong relationship with that prospect.

e) You know the prospect's buying process.

f) You know the prospect has the budget.

Education—The customer knows that your product or service will exceed their expectations, and the customer is inspired to take action to obtain the product or service.

Agreement—During or at the end of the Agreement step, the customer has firmly decided to buy and has voiced that decision.

Closing—The result of the Closing step is the successful transition of the prospect from the salesperson to the delivery team. This includes all the final logistics and paperwork required to finalize the sale. This frees up the salesperson to completely focus on the sales process with another prospective customer. Attention is no longer tied up in the worry of whether or not the previous customer will be taken care of.

These are the eight key steps of the sales process. Your individual sales processes may have finer adjustments, but these are the basic steps.

Important note: the most vital part of this chapter is that each step has a *result*. *The quality of the result at each step determines how easy or hard the transition to the next step will be.* The salesperson, by focusing on each step and clearly seeing the results *they* are achieving, builds momentum during the process on the way to closing.

Remember the earlier statement that motivation is tied to results. This is how salespeople create and maintain their own motivation. If you find you are losing motivation, review the sales you have in process to determine what step you have truly completed. Knowing where you truly are in each sales process is a relief and gives you clear direction with the next step to take! With this process in place, you are now empowered to troubleshoot why a sale is not closing, leading to higher closing rates. During the pilot phase of the sales process, salespeople referred to this new technology as the "holy grail" they had been searching for.

By running each sale this way, you may find that your abilities are stronger in some steps and weaker in others. *Knowing* this is the start of becoming a master salesperson. The key is the continuous improvement of your sales abilities (SELLability).

What are the core abilities you need to develop in order to master the sales process? What are the skills required to master each of these abilities? After we researched and re-engineered the sales process, we turned our focus to the abilities the top 20% of salespeople had in common.

We isolated 8 consistent abilities that made the top 20% of salespeople effective at each step of the sales process. In SELL-ability we named these the "8 Core Abilities." To solve 80/20 we realized that we had to provide a program to continuously improve the skills required to master these abilities.

The first goal is to have you learn and follow the re-engi-neered sales process so that it becomes second nature. The second goal is to help you develop the skills needed to *master* the 8 core abilities required to be effective at each step of the sales process.

The next chapter is dedicated to these 8 Core Abilities.

1.PROSPECTING:

PROSPECTING MUST INCLUDE AN EFFECTIVE PUBLIC RELATIONS CAMPAIGN RESULTING IN YOUR COMPANY BEING A VALUABLE, TRUSTED SOURCE OF INFORMATION FOR YOUR MARKET.

Prospecting Result
Focus on being a "Trusted Source of Information".

A trusted source of information.

Prospecting result: You've developed a huge database of potential prospects of the public that will buy your products or services. You have provided that public with valuable free content, keeping them actively in communication with your company resulting in your company being considered a valuable source of information AND a company the prospects can TRUST! With that in place, you can now research, and then contact those public and develop them into prospects who will smoothly go into communication at the contact step and move through your sales process.

2. MARKETING CAMPAIGN:
A Marketing Campaign Can Now Be Effective To The Prospects Who Already Trust You.

3. ABUNDANCE OF QUALIFIED PROSPECTS RESPONDING AND REACHING FOR YOUR PRODUCTS AND SERVICES:

MASTER THE SALES PROCESS
MASTER RESULTS & MOTIVATION/RETENTION

3

THE 8 CORE ABILITIES – 8 C'S OF SELLING

Now that we've covered the sales process in detail, let's cover the abilities required to effectively guide a prospect through that process.

In our research, we discovered that all successful salespeople —yes, that top 20 percent—have 8 core abilities in common. In our SELLability and 80/20 Sales Technology, we have isolated these abilities and call them *The 8-Cs of Selling*. These are the abilities used to guide someone through the sales process we just covered. Every salesperson must master them.

The 8 core abilities work together. You need to master all 8 core abilities to be successful in the sales process.

SELLability's   8 Core Abilities:

1. COMMUNICATION
An effortless ability to establish agreement with anyone and build trust. The salesperson knows the right questions to ask targeting a prospect's TRUE MOTIVATIONS.

2. CONTROL
The salesperson no longer feels Control is manupulative, rather it's used to steer the prospect in the right direction using INTENTION and a step-by-step sales process.

3. CONTACT
The salesperson knows that he or she MUST GET ATTENTION to stand out from the competition. The salesperson has learned to have a fearless approach to getting in front of the right prospects.

4. CERTAINTY
The salesperson knows their product or service's benefits (and limitations) flawlessly, and knows how to HANDLE AND DIFFUSE any prospect resistance.

5. CONFIDENCE
The salesperson can "READ" PROSPECT'S emotional traits, including spotting not only the time wasters, but by never missing buying signals. They are also trained to make an EMOTIONAL impact for their product or service.

6. COMPETENCE
The salesperson uses customized "IMPINGEMENT MARKETING COLLATERAL" to help make the case for their product, and ethically destroy the competition.

7. CLOSING
With a clear understanding of how to BUILD VALUE for their product or service they close deals effortlessly, at higher margins.

8. CUSTOMER RELATIONSHIP
The salesperson never misses an opportunity to WIN REFERRALS at the right time. Their current and past clients are loyal to a fault and help drive their new business.

CORE ABILITY #1 - COMMUNICATION

Communication is the effortless ability to establish agreement with anyone and build trust. It is the ability to get the prospect to talk and to then, through a better understanding of human relationships, help change the prospect's mind. It is the most basic and important of the salesperson skills.

CHANGING A VIEWPOINT REQUIRES UNDERSTANDING

In order to change someone's point of view, you must first understand *their* point of view. A fantastic example of this is the kid whose room is a total mess. The parent walks in and says, "This room is a mess!" But whose point of view is that? The parent's point of view! Do parents in this situation ever ask the kid what he thinks of his room?

What the parent fails to do in selling the child to clean their room, is to understand the kid's point of view. Quite likely, the kid thinks the room is perfect. He probably feels he knows where everything is and wants his room this way. In such a case, getting the kid to clean up his room would be a tough sell.

The first step to convincing the kid to clean their room would be to understand what they think about their room. Have the kid take the parent on a tour of the room and tell the parent what the kid sees from *their* point of view.

This would take patience that most parents, unfortunately, don't have—and most salespeople don't have that patience, either. They just want to close the sale. Using communication skills to really understand the customer's point of view is vital to establishing trust.

COMMUNICATION AND UNDERSTANDING GO TOGETHER

If you cannot communicate well, you're never going to find out what people need and want, and what products or services you can sell them. You're never going to get anywhere near the close.

People can fall into one of several categories when it comes to communication. Some can be really good at listening, which is a definite plus. Others can be compulsive talkers, which is really something you want to get over if you're going to succeed in sales. Yet others rush through communication because they're unsure of how to handle it, or are trying to avoid it.

Most salespeople consider themselves great communicators. We haven't found that to be the case, though, and the primary barrier to acquiring great communication skills is believing you have nothing else to learn about them. So no matter your level of skill, the first thing you should decide is that there is something you can learn about communication.

COMMUNICATION RELATES DIRECTLY TO THE SALES PROCESS

The core ability of communication relates to each step of the sales process. Think about how good your communication skills must be in the Prospecting step, given the tens of thousands of messages they are already receiving.

In prospecting through the internet you are also communicating to prospects you have never had a *live* conversation with. This is a *big* challenge.

What you're doing in the Research step is gathering further data to effectively communicate in the Contact and Interview step.

In the Contact and Interview step, you need to be a good listener, and understand the customer's point of view.

In the Qualifying step, it's your communication skills that will pull out the vital information you need from the prospect.

You'll use great communication to Educate the prospect and to gain their agreement to buy.

In Closing, it is your communication skill that will make for a smooth transition from the salesperson to the delivery team.

COMMUNICATION SKILLS IN THE DIGITAL AGE

Salespeople are often champions of technology and communicating through devices. Therefore, it is worthwhile taking up modern devices as they relate to communication.

When speaking on the topic of communication, we are often asked this question: *"Did modern digital technology improve communication skills?"* While modern devices did increase our ability to communicate faster and more efficiently, did the recent generations, growing up in the digital age, grow up with increased communication skills?

Our generation was lucky enough to experience life *with* and *without* technology, and there are definitely differences.

When I (Nick) was a kid, I lived in a small farming community with little to no technology—a TV was a luxury for sure. Everyone in our community knew each other. My mother was a nurse, so if someone needed help in the community they knew to call her or come to our home.

We also raised chickens and provided eggs to the neighborhood, and my first real job was collecting eggs. We traded those eggs to the other farmers for pork and beef.

The community worked together. We really knew each other and we were in *real communication* with each other. Asking a neighbor to borrow some flour or sugar or a tool was no problem—in fact, it was expected. If we needed help to build a fence or fix something in the house, it was no problem. We learned to use communication as a necessity for survival at a very early age.

These skills improved as we grew up and were maintained throughout life. I would say that for generations before mine, the necessity to communicate was even greater.

Now let's look at recent generations, our children included. Today's digital technology allows us to communicate through devices instead of with each other. Social media allows us to interact without having *real* communication or *real* understanding of each other—just ask yourself, "How many of my Facebook friends do I truly know and trust?"

There are more issues associated with our digital society. Video gaming dominates leisure time so there are fewer community functions, keeping us further out of communication. There is increasing conflict pushed into society through media outlets and social media, causing mistrust and fear, shutting down communication even further.

KNOW YOUR NEIGHBOR, KNOW YOUR PROSPECT

Answer this question for yourself: "How well do we really know and understand each other?" When was the last time you went to a neighbor to borrow something? Food, supplies, a tool?

It's interesting—and, factually, sad—that it almost takes a tragedy to bring us back together. After 9/11 in the United

States, the country came together, even if only for a short time. It brought the international community together as well.

In California, where we live, fires came close enough to wipe out the houses in our neighborhood—and suddenly there was a necessity to really meet each other because our survival depended on it.

This pattern needs to change. We do need to meet and understand each other—in our neighborhoods, in our communities, in our companies, and in society as a whole. Practice meeting people, using good manners and granting them importance.

You may find out that while people really want to know each other, they are fearful and do not trust each other easily. We propose we work on this together. A little "old-school" may be just what is needed!

COMMUNICATION IN OUR COMMUNITY TRANSFERS TO BETTER SALES ABILITY

Now, how does this relate to sales? In our research, we found that the decline in communication skills outside of the office directly relates to the 80/20 law in sales—especially in the sales process steps of Prospecting, Research, Contact and Interview, and Qualifying. In fact, the reason for 80/20 lies in the fact that those 4 steps aren't being done. If we are not effectively using communication skills with our friends, families, and communities, we are not likely successful in our sales process.

When you look at the areas of sales and customer service, have they improved or are they getting worse over time? We noted earlier that one solution to the lack of sales skills and customer service has been to move sales online, removing the human element from the sales process.

While there is some value in this move for some products, most of us would rather deal with a person we trust when buying a product or service. We also want to experience these products and services ourselves, not just see pictures of them online. At some point, the issue of communication skills will have to be addressed out of necessity.

This is good news for you and your company. Imagine if you and your team were all masters of communication, customer service, and sales. How would this change your company or life? How would this change neighborhoods, communities, and companies? Don't overthink the problem, but instead focus on improving the communication skills of you and your team.

TRULY LISTENING VS. PRETENDING

A primary skill in communication, especially in sales and customer service, is listening.

We discovered that many people when they're supposedly listening, are actually thinking about what they're going to say next. You're not actually paying attention to the conversation if you're thinking about something else.

You should really and truly *listen*. If you're not really listening, you're missing things that are going to help you complete each step of the sales process.

Listening is critical to ensuring you get the result of each sales process step. If you examine a failure to achieve each step of the sales process, it always relates directly to listening to and understanding what your prospect is saying.

While you're listening, you might want to take notes. Not only will doing so assist you later in recalling important details of the meeting, but it's part of granting importance to your prospect. It shows that what they're saying is important to you. This does require some judgment—you don't want to be writing so much that it distracts from the conversation. It also depends on the type of sale. You can also bring a little recorder with you and ask the person if you can record the conversation, if applicable.

Listening and being interested will cause you to ask more questions, based on your understanding. If you're really not understanding the customer, then you can fail to follow up with important questions. For example, the customer may tell you an important piece of information, but a detail might be missing. If you're listening and paying attention, you're going to follow that up.

THE AWKWARD SILENCE

There's an aspect of listening that is a common failing in sales communication, and we haven't discovered anyone who didn't have trouble with it. It is the awkward silence. That is, when there's a pause in the communication, when the prospect is thinking something over, for example, the salesperson feels compelled to communicate and fill that silence. This is something you should never do. The salesperson should have the patience to allow the customer to finish their thought.

We can't count the number of times we've been right at the close of a very big deal and when we ask for the close, there's an awkward silence. The first instinct can be to cut out the awkward silence and say something. In fact, the majority of people we have worked with tend to have a million things going through their minds, such as "Maybe I should lower the price" or "Maybe I should offer a discount."

It is essential that you force yourself to be quiet and just wait for the prospect to speak. In doing so, most people find that they get the close, and have even found that a prospect would add to the deal! The awkward silence was there because the prospect was considering what they wanted to add to the purchase.

GET THE PROSPECT TO TELL YOU WHAT THEY TRULY THINK

You must become masters at the art of granting importance to the customer and staying interested in them and what they are saying. Because you grant enough importance to their thoughts, their feelings, and what they're thinking, and stay interested in the prospect and their ideas, the customer wants to communicate even more.

As we covered in detail in the last chapter, the fundamental duty of a salesperson is to establish trust with the prospect so that they tell you what they're truly thinking. The communication aspect of this is getting the prospect to talk.

Getting the prospect to talk is done by granting importance to the prospect and what they're saying and continuing to be interested—asking them, for example, to tell you more about that.

The key here is to be genuine—if you're not genuine, the customer is going to know that, too. But if you're genuinely interested in them and their ideas, they'll want to communicate more.

If you don't do that, you never learn anything about their needs, wants, and desires as they relate to what you're selling. As a result, there is no sales process, no close.

ASSUMING IS A DANGEROUS GAME

If you're really sharp, you can sometimes spot a person's issues or problems without them saying what they are. But this is highly dangerous, as it's assuming and we all know what assuming does.

In spite of the fact that *you* spot these issues, you still must guide the customer to say it themselves. If *they* say it, it's true, but if you say it, they can always argue with you. Get the *prospect* to tell you. Under the Contact section below, we'll provide you some sample questions to get a person to open up.

We recall a particularly large deal, about 10 years ago. It was worth several million dollars, but even more over the next 5 years. We had spent months and months creating the trust and desire to work with our company.

We had agreed on all the terms and were just finalizing details when we made the mistake of verbalizing why the prospect should go with a particular type of computer system. We had discussed it earlier, but he had not verbalized it himself.

By us saying it, we gave the prospect something to argue about. We spent hours making up for that. In the end, the prospect verbalized his problems exactly, per his point of view, and the type of systems he should get. The deal closed but we learned our lesson for sure!

WELCOME OBJECTIONS INSTEAD OF AVOIDING THEM

There is much to be said about objections in sales and we cover the topic throughout this book. There is most definitely a communication aspect to it: you have to be willing to *face* objections head-on and talk about them, and even invite the prospect to bring them up. This takes communication skills, so when we talk about mastering communication skills and mastering the sales process, by doing that you are going to be able to master handling objections.

Don't go into a sales cycle afraid of getting an objection. Don't get the idea that if you don't talk about it, it isn't really there—it will be! If your prospect has an objection, and you don't bring it out into the open and at least discuss it, it will still be there at the end of the meeting, and it could very well kill the sale.

Of course, you can err in the other direction, and try to second-guess a prospect, throwing out a common objection before the prospect does. This is not a good practice, why put an objection in the prospect's mind that may never have been there in the first place? We have found that one of the reasons for sales failure in the 80/20 law is putting objections in the prospect's mind that weren't there.

NO PRECONCEPTIONS

An expansion on that last point is, don't go into a sales cycle with any preconceived ideas of what is going to happen. Think for a moment: have you ever had the idea that someone was about to say one thing, and what actually came out of their mouth was something altogether different? Remember that when you're selling. Let the person talk until they have said everything they're going to say. This way you grant them importance while taking time to fully understand what they're expressing.

Note that one of the critical reasons to follow a sales process is that each prospect requires their own unique sales process. Understanding and following a sales process allows you to be more alert and to individualize the details along the way. Although you're following the same sales process steps

every time, the details of each step of the process and the customer's viewpoint in each process are totally different and you should treat them that way. This grants each prospect the importance they deserve.

RE-FOCUS BETWEEN EACH SALES PROCESS

If a sales process goes badly, you may have had an unqualified prospect. Step back, look at that sales process and see where it went wrong. Then, shift your attention off of it by deciding what you will do next. You refocus anew and go onto the next sale.

For example, if you spot in the sale that went wrong that you need to do more to develop trust, make a note of that for your next meeting with that prospect, and move on.

Dragging an unfinished sale-gone-wrong into a whole new sales process is going to create a disaster because your attention is still on what went wrong.

The steps are the same with a closed sale—if you've just closed a sale, and you now need to make that transition to the delivery team (as covered in the last chapter), make an appointment to do so. This takes your attention off of it as you move onto your next sales process.

We've seen it too many times: a salesperson gets a close and the next prospect doesn't seem very important because they just got a close! If you're going to eventually close 80 percent of your sales, refocusing your attention is vital.

In the end, people buy your product or service, to a large degree, based on how much they like, respect, and trust you. This is often a more important factor than the product itself and it stems completely from your communication skills.

CORE ABILITY #2 - CONTROL

GUIDING AND CARING IS KEY FOR CONTROL

Selling successfully isn't about winging it and hoping for the best. It requires *control*—the ability to positively guide your client in the right direction. It includes caring enough to maintain the discipline necessary to successfully present your product or service using a predetermined sales process, which we covered in the last chapter.

If you genuinely care about your prospect, you will follow each step of the sales process, guiding them to buy the product which is why they came to see you or called you.

Remember, they wouldn't have reached out to you unless they were interested. People don't have the time to waste these days. If they communicate with you, they're interested. Your key is to use positive control and guide them through the process, caring enough about them to get them through to a close.

A salesperson should not feel that control is manipulative or a bad thing. What the majority of salespeople do not understand is that most buyers love, even crave, positive control. They *want* to be guided through the process. We all do! We want to meet the expert of that product or service and then be positively guided through the process.

POSITIVE CONTROL VS. NEGATIVE OR BAD PAST EXPERIENCE

Many business owners, salespeople, and people, in general, have a distaste for the idea of control. This is usually due to

bad control experiences in their lives. When we're talking about control, we're not talking about bad control or a bad experience. We don't mean being rude, pushy, or in any way offensive.

We're talking about using good communication skills to discover the prospect's goals, their dreams, their interests, and the problems they're looking to solve, in association with what it is they're looking to buy. Guiding someone through the process is easier when you're totally certain that your product or service is a fit for the prospect.

So, guiding them through the process is guiding them to the point where they realize, and you as the salesperson realize, that your product or service is a perfect match for them. By both of you realizing that, we end up with the perfect definition for a sale: **an exchange in which both parties win.**

STAYING TRUE TO THE SALES PROCESS
WITHOUT COMPROMISE

As discussed earlier, we thoroughly created and tested our sales process, and used it ourselves in every sale to see how it worked.

The sales process provides a very necessary degree of control for the salesperson in bringing about the sale. We do know of what we speak; we have lived this sales process successfully. We feel blessed that we can now present it to the masses and help change the 80/20 rule. We can help almost everyone be a top salesperson!

We remember a time way back when we were pilot testing our sales process. We had completed years of research with trial and error. We were on the phone with a high-level potential client who had called in upon receiving a promotion. We immediately pulled up the sales process app we created and began following it as we discussed the prospect's situation.

It was a good test of the SELLability sales process and app. The potential client we were talking to was in a hurry and was pushing us in all directions. We were doing our best to stick to the sales process, while the prospect kept demanding "The price! I want the price! Can we just get to the price?"

We politely acknowledged him every time he did something like that, saying, "Yes, that's very important, and we're going to address that! " We've noted this down and we'll get to it."

We continued through the sales process and the sale closed. Afterward, the prospect told us that he really appreciated the fact that we listened and addressed all of his concerns.

We could have done what many salespeople do—become flustered and jump off the sales process trying to answer all the prospect's questions, going in every direction, thinking that if we didn't, the prospect would think we were not addressing them. This would have been a serious mistake.

THE SALES PROCESS HAS LAYERS LIKE AN ONION

You could view the potential sale as an onion and the sales process as carefully peeling off the layers of the onion, one by one, in as comfortable a manner as possible. At the core of the onion is the prospect's goal. The prospect is trying to get there but doesn't know how. So they've come to you to help guide them.

During the sale, the prospect may demand that you address the 4th layer when you're still on the 1st. You can't because you've got to carefully peel off those first 3 layers to get there.

By all means, note down what the prospect says and let them know you've done so and will take it up in due course. But, *stay with the sales process*. Make sure to get every layer of that onion completely dealt with before moving on to the next.

One of the things we often do at this point is to ask the prospect if they've ever had a bad buying experience. Of course, the prospect replies "Yes!" You can then say, "So have I!" You can let them know that "One of the differences in our company is that we do a thorough interview. At the end of this interview, both you and I are going to know if my products and services are a match for you. If they are, we'll

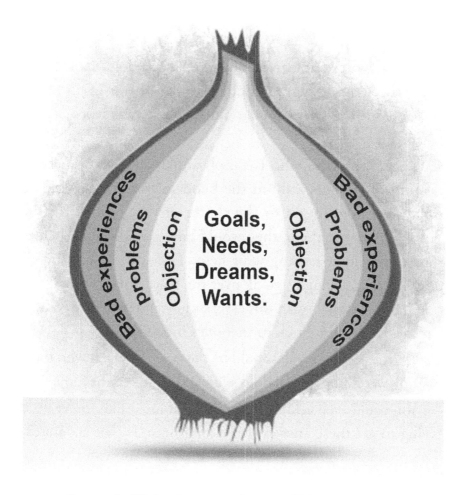

move forward. If they're not, then we'll both know that. Is that fair?" A prospect can't help but agree. This will usually lower their resistance.

You could even say at this point, "The reason we do it this way is that we really care about you. We're not a company simply focused on a sale. We actually expect you to be a customer for life." That will normally calm the prospect down, reduce sales resistance, and allow you to follow your sales process, which is critical.

SELLING TO THE DOMINANT CLIENT PERSONALITY

The above example was one example of a dominant client, with whom a salesperson could play tug-of-war in an effort to stay with the sales process. There are several types of this personality.

There's the type who is simply impatient, who has been beating themselves around the bend for months, trying to figure out how to get to the center of that onion. If they knew how to get there, they would have done so long before they came along seeking your help. They can be frustrated, domineering, trying to go all over the place, and *appear* like a dominant personality. In this case, simply and patiently control the sale, as we did. Stick to that sales process.

Or, the prospect really could be the type of person who must control everything. You should still handle the sale the same way.

You could even acknowledge, "Hey, it looks like you've been trying to get these answers for a long time. Is that accurate?" The prospect will most likely agree, "Yes!" You can then say, "No matter what, my job is to take care of you as a customer, provide you with a little bit of customer service so that in the end you'll have all the answers, which was the reason you set this appointment."

At that point, if it seems like my product is a match, both from my point of view *and* from your point of view, we could move forward. If it isn't a match, it's totally okay. At least then you'll have your questions answered, I will have provided you with a service, and this meeting will not have been a waste of your time. Is that fair?"

No matter what, don't fear the dominant client personality. Most of the time such people have a goal in mind and just don't know quite how to reach it. That's where you come in. Be patient and, again, stick to that sales process.

Acknowledge what the prospect is thinking.
In order to do that you must listen and encourage them to tell you what they are thinking.
Acknowledgement is key to positive control throughout the sales process.

CORE ABILITY #3 - CONTACT

HAVE NO FEAR OR DOUBT YOU WILL MAKE CONTACT

What is the skill of contacting, for a salesperson? It's the salesperson's *ability to have a fearless approach to getting in front of the right prospect.*

The ability to contact ties right in with something we go through with our clients all the time. Visiting a client's sales department, we'll hear from sales reps that they're having trouble getting people on the phone.

One salesperson might say that they've been trying to reach an important prospect for three days and just can't reach them. One of us will calmly walk over, dial the phone, and have the prospect answer. They think that we have some mystical, magic ability, but we'll tell you that it was only our strong *intention* (decision) to reach that person.

We would then go back to the salesperson and would sit down with them to isolate exactly *why* they were not reaching people. There is always a reason, and it has everything to do with the person doing the calling. What is the salesperson afraid the prospect is going to say that the salesperson won't be prepared to answer?

Our experience revealed this: 90 percent of the skill of contacting, getting in front of the right qualified people, is being prepared, and having enough confidence in making that call. Being prepared means having completed research and knowing exactly who you're calling, as per the sales process.

Confidence comes in your communication skills discussed earlier, plus knowing how to start a conversation and how to get agreement, which we'll cover later in this book.

WORRIES OR DOUBTS COME FROM PAST FAILURES TO CONTACT

The only reason salespeople don't want to reach other people is because they've had a bad experience in reaching people earlier. It comes back to the salesperson resisting the prospect's resistance. So, if you're a master at handling resistance and breaking it down, you're not going to have a problem contacting people.

The reason we're so successful in reaching people is that we're very interested in people. People are interesting. One of the best things about a sales job is meeting people. If you don't like people or are afraid to talk to people, you're going to have a hard time mastering the Contact skill.

One way to clear up a salesperson's worries about reaching someone is to have them tell you if they've had a bad experience selling to someone. Have them tell you all about it. If a salesperson has had a high degree of resistance, they become less and less interested in talking to people. You may need to clean that up with salespeople, and even with yourself, on a regular basis.

FOCUS ON CLOSING KILLS CONTACT CONFIDENCE

Another reason we found salespeople have a hard time reaching people is that, from the very beginning, they have anxiety about trying to close. As soon as they get rid of the idea that they have to close from the beginning, the salesperson calms down and begins to focus on each sales process step, which ultimately helps them slide right into the close at the end.

The easy way to close is to focus on each of the steps of the sales process. First is the Research step; once you've accomplished that, you should be interested in talking to that person. So, now you're going to do the Contact and Interview step, and so on.

Following the sales process reduces the anxiety salespeople have around closing. Again, closing happens at the end, and

rushing to the close contributes to the 80/20 phenomenon. By refocusing the salesperson onto the beginning steps of the sales process, the anxiety salespeople had about contacting prospects is greatly reduced.

GETTING YOUR PROSPECT TO TALK TO YOU

One problem new salespeople can face is getting someone they don't know talking, which is of course vital to the sales process. You might get lucky and encounter someone who is social and likes to talk, but more often, as with a cold call, you're going to contact someone who just wants to get off the phone.

Note that if you follow the Research step of the sales process, you don't really need to do a cold call.

SELLABILITY'S RULE OF 8

SELLability's Rule of 8 provides you with an 8-step key to getting a prospect talking and unlocking early-stage sales resistance.

The Rule of 8:

1. Use good manners and etiquette: a vital necessity in sales.

   Et-i-quette Noun \ 'e-ti-kət, - ket\: the rules indicating the proper and polite way to behave (including appearance)

2. Grant importance: show respect, awareness of their position and/or experience.

   Note: This step does not always have to be verbal. Feel free to contact SELLability (SELLability.com) for more information.

3. Establish agreement: what can you both agree on?
4. Discover interest: what motivated or inspired them to call, to take your call, or to visit with you?
5. Address prior prospect experience: any prior experience (s) with this product or service, or a product or service similar to yours?
6. Envision the future: what are their future expectations in regard to this product or service?
7. Get an up-front agreement: if I can show how this product or service would save you time and/or money and solve _____ problem, would you be willing to move forward?
8. Continue to QUALIFY as you begin to PRESENT.

RULE OF 8

CONTACT	INTERVIEW
1.MANNERS	5.PRIOR EXPERIENCE
2.GRANTING IMPORTANCE	6.FUTURE VISION
3.ESTABLISHING AGREEMENT	7.UPFRONT AGREEMENT
4.DISCOVER INTEREST = REAL COMMUNICATION	8.CONTINUING TO QUALIFY =CREATE ENOUGH TRUST THAT THE CUSTOMER TELLS YOU WHAT YOU NEED TO KNOW TO FULLY COMPLETE THE QUALIFY STEP

Here are some sample questions to get someone talking:
• What motivated you to inquire about _____ today?
• What inspired you to call (or make this appointment) today?

- Tell me about your interest in our product or service.
- How long have you been thinking about buying _____?
- May I ask what prevented you from moving forward or buying before now?
- Have you ever used _____ like this one?
- What are you trying to achieve?
- What has been your past experience with a similar product or service?
- How long have you had this problem?
- What problems have you experienced using a similar product or service?
- What are you trying to achieve?
- What prevented you from purchasing it so far?
- What would the ideal product or service do for you?

If you spend a little time at it, you can come up with some of your own questions to get people talking that tie in with the products and services you sell.

WEAK PRODUCT OR SERVICE KNOWLEDGE LEADS TO CONTACT FAILURES

In analyzing why a salesperson was uncertain about talking to prospects, we often discovered the salesperson wasn't totally certain about their product or service.

Every salesperson should spend regular time studying up on what they're selling—not just on features and benefits, but really how it works and what makes it tick.

You can role-play with someone else asking you random questions, just like a prospect would. In order to get real scenarios, this is best role-played with someone who has experience answering such questions.

Whenever you're uncertain about contacting, dig in and figure out why. Get that sorted out and *then* reach out to contact prospects. You'll find that you have much better luck reaching people and that you have smoother conversations.

When training salespeople, we will sometimes take them out to see a customer who is using the product or service the salesperson will be selling. This way, the salesperson can see firsthand the benefits the customer is experiencing. It gives the salesperson confidence in the product. What are the different ways they're using it? What are the benefits they see from it? What do they love about it?

It also works well to have a customer call in once a week to share a testimonial on your product or service, or leave a recorded message for the staff to be played as part of the staff meeting.

It's very motivating to know that what you're selling is actually being used and that using your product or service has been a win for your customers. This certainly provides motivation for contacting the next prospect. The key is to find endless examples of how your product is being used and how it's changing people's lives.

"ALWAYS BE CONTACTING"

Traditionally, the "ABCs" of sales has meant "Always Be Closing." As demonstrated in this book, as well as many other SELLability materials, this is a totally wrong approach.

Therefore, let's redefine the "ABCs" of sales as "Always Be Contacting"- a motto we have lived by and have had incredible success with.

THE HP ADVENTURE

At one time, we had been trying for months to get in contact with a particular person in a particular division in Hewlett-Packard. We had tried just about everything—writing letters, reaching out through all our other contacts for a possible introduction, attending networking events—none of the conventional methods had worked.

Finally, we just announced to our staff one day, during a staff meeting, that we'd been trying to reach this particular executive for six weeks and had exhausted all our resources. We asked if anyone had any thoughts or ideas on how to reach them.

After the meeting, one of the staff approached us and told us that her brother-in-law worked for the person we were trying to reach. The moral of this particular story is that nothing is off the table when it comes to trying to reach someone. Be creative!

STRATEGIC ALLIANCE ADVENTURE

It might be that I (Lisa) am so good at making contacts because I was dumped into the deep end of the pool fairly early in my career. At a software company I worked for, I was charged with establishing a Strategic Alliances Division, which had never been done at that company. I was literally starting with no contacts, no staff…and no budget.

Just after obtaining this position, I found out about a seminar being given about the very subject I was interested in: creating strategic alliance relationships. I happily traveled to this seminar and sat as close to the panel delivering the seminar as I could. During the Q&A session, I asked how I would make contacts in this field without having any. I was told to talk to one of them after the seminar.

When I did, I was invited to spend $25,000, and for that fee, this particular person would make introductions for me to 10 of his contacts. This didn't include any kind of help towards closing a deal or even getting a meeting set up. It was only for an introduction. Needless to say, with no budget, I couldn't do it, but the experience did bring home the importance of having great contacts and relationships.

I then became obsessed with getting the contacts I needed—I had been told, and I believed, that my company's future depended on it. I went at it from every possible angle. I hand-wrote letters and sent them by mail. I called a person's office and sweet-talked the receptionist into giving me an email address.

If that didn't work, I would look through the company's website, noting any email address I found as most companies in those days had standard email address conventions for their personnel, such as first name, last name initial@company. com. I'd then adapt that convention for the person I was trying to reach.

I'd even go to the "contact us" page of the website, which in those days was usually for tech support, and put my entire letter there, with a note at the top to "Please forward this." I would also try, of course, just calling the company and seeing if I could get through to the person. I also attended every networking event I could.

Through every method imaginable, I went after every contact I could and I got them! The strategy certainly worked and I was eventually promoted out of that position to be CEO of the company.

ALWAYS BE RESPECTFUL—THE AIRPORT ADVENTURE

Anyone who has done a lot of traveling has had the occasional bad experience with delayed flights. Generally, passengers are greatly disgruntled at this and tend to not be nice, even to each other.

We were once in the midst of such an experience, having had a particular flight delayed three times and counting. Almost everyone was swearing, yelling, and being disrespectful and rude. There was a man sitting next to us—we had been sitting next to each other for hours working on our laptops.

Finally, the man looked at us and said, "You've got to be the nicest people on the planet! This plane has been delayed so many times I can't even count. Everyone here is stark-raving mad or about to murder someone. And you're just the most polite, sincere people ever!"

We thanked the man, and we started talking. He turned out to be a senior VP at IBM, and we had been trying to get in touch with a senior VP there for several months. This man was at our disposal for several more hours while we waited for the plane and we were able to have the conversation we'd been trying to have for months and we actually started conducting business right there.

This all happened because of how we took care to carry and present ourselves in all situations. Many people wouldn't even care about being respectful or using manners in such a situation—after all, they're not there to meet people. But as we found out, you never know who you're going to meet.

THE RESTAURANT ADVENTURE

Another time, we were with some clients at a restaurant in Las Vegas during an enormous trade show headed by Microsoft. The tables in this restaurant were close to each other, so we ended up talking to a couple at the next table.

We were having such a great time that we moved the tables closer to each other and spent the rest of the evening together.

At the end of the evening, the man said, "By the way, if you have any interest in meeting Bill Gates or Steve Ballmer [the CEO and President of Microsoft at the time], let me know." We said that of course ,we'd be interested! The man then said, "I don't normally tell anyone or invite anyone like that. But you haven't asked me once for any kind of contact or favor. I can see that you're really nice people, and that's the kind of people they like doing business with."

Turned out the man was Bill Gates' bodyguard!

THE MICROSOFT CAMPUS ADVENTURE

On another occasion, we were visiting the Microsoft campus. We were at our hotel, in a long line of people to get a taxi. While in line, we'd been standing next to a man, casually talking. A short time later, another man came along, and he and the man we had been speaking with began talking, it was obvious they knew each other. The man who had come up asked where we were going. We were going to the Microsoft campus. The man said he was going there as well. He had his car and offered us a ride.

On the way to Microsoft, we told the man who was driving about our company and product, and about our company's long-term relationship with Microsoft. When we arrived at the Microsoft campus, the man parked his car. It turned out he was going to the same building we were going to. He asked who we were there to see, and we told him.

He then said, "Oh, she works for me!" The man ended up introducing us to the woman with the line, "Take really good care of these people." We are friends to this day.

AGAIN—ALWAYS BE CONTACTING

We can circle back around to the statement at the beginning of this section: **Always Be Contacting!** In today's world, in which bad manners are the norm, having great manners and being respectful will get you a long way.

We recommend being a great person all the time, not just when you need a contact, which has certainly worked well for us. By operating this way, many of the contacts we were trying and trying to reach had a tendency to find their way *to us*.

CORE ABILITY #4 - CERTAINTY

WHAT, PRECISELY, IS CERTAINTY?

Believe it or not, certainty is what buyers buy. Prospects buy certainty. They have come for the appointment or called your company because they want to be guided through the sales process. They have an interest, and they're not totally certain. They've done their homework, as most prospects do these days—they've talked to their friends, they've searched on the internet—but they still have questions.

They're now looking for somebody to guide them through the process, to answer those final questions so they can buy that product or service.

It is the salesperson who knows their product or service flawlessly and knows how to handle prospect resistance. They are also totally professional and masters of their company's sales process.

BE A GUIDE THAT IS TRULY KNOWLEDGEABLE

Certainty also consists of knowing as much as possible about your prospect, their company, and their line of products and services. This certainty will cause that salesperson to strictly follow their sales process and to learn all about their prospect.

If, for example, you're selling a life insurance product, know all there is to know about it and its benefits. Know the

Master salesperson who is certain | Amateur who is uncertain

history as well. In selling life insurance, the easiest opening question to any potential prospect is, "When do people think about life insurance?"

The most common answer is going to be when there is a life-changing event, a tragedy, something that reminds them that they need it and by then it's going to be too late.

In making contact, the first point of certainty for the life insurance salesperson is knowing, with certainty, that every person needs life insurance and has thought about it. When have they thought about it? When some disastrous occurrence reminded them of it.

Given all the different events that occur, either in our own lives or people's lives we read about or hear about, people have thought about life insurance more than once in the last two weeks. Life insurance salespeople should have no problem finding prospects.

Equally as important, learn all about competing products and services so you can intelligently discuss them and why yours would be more of an advantage for your prospect. Then, learn as much about your prospect, their particular circumstances, and what they would need from you.

All of this takes certainty. Certainty also comes from experience, meeting with, and gaining interest from lots of prospects. We have discovered the top 20 percent of salespeople are certain because they are interested and ask their prospects lots of questions. They learn more and more about their prospects, their point of view, and what they are interested in. They continue to be professionals at presenting their products and services in relation to the prospect's needs, which they learn from the prospects themselves. That's really what provides certainty.

IT'S A WORLD OF EDUCATED BUYERS

It used to be that the salesperson was the expert on a product or service, to whom a prospect would listen because they didn't really have any other source of information. With the creation of the internet, however, buyers can learn as much as you about your product and service...and about your competitors' products, too.

By the time they contact you, they have already formed opinions and may have even made at least a partial decision on which product they will purchase. You've got to be ready by having that *certainty.* That certainty comes from being more educated than your potential prospect, both about your product and your competition.

THERE ARE 8 KEY ABILITIES AND TOOLS THAT ADD UP TO SALES CERTAINTY:

1. Mastering the sales process: Know each step. Practice and drill to be fully professional. Complete each step.
2. Mastering the 8C's (The 8 Core Abilities of Selling): These abilities create certainty to get a prospect through the sales process.
3. Master communication skills: This is the foundation for success in both key abilities one and two, above.
4. Know your own products and services: Especially know why your company is the best. Knowing client case studies is vital.
5. Know all about competing products and services and what makes yours better.

6. Know the FAQs: Knowing answers to the frequently asked questions gives confidence to the prospect.

7. Master handling objections: Welcome objections without anxiety and smoothly handle them.

8. Know and effectively use marketing and sales collateral: This tool is a real support to your presentation. Prospects believe what is in writing.

In the end, you need to have no attention on yourself or what you're saying. Have no attention on your ability to answer any questions or handle any scenario your prospect might bring up.

CORE ABILITY #5 - CONFIDENCE

CONFIDENCE COMES FROM LEARNING AND APPLICATION

Confidence comes from being a master at all 8 Core Abilities and truly being a master of the sales process. If you were truly a master of the 8 core abilities as well as being a master of the sales process, you'd certainly have a lot of confidence.

Confidence is not arrogance. If prospects sense your confidence, they are encouraged to buy. They are there to buy anyway, but they are looking for a confident, professional salesperson to guide them through the process.

Confidence means that the salesperson totally understands each step of the sales process. Confidence means the salesperson understands the prospects' emotions and understands that the prospect probably had previous bad buying experiences, which causes resistance to the sales process.

Sales person being confident and positive melting resistance.

Sales person not being confident and increasing resistance in the prospect.

KNOW THE BUYING PROCESS
FROM THE PROSPECT'S VIEWPOINT

Confidence stems from the understanding that the buying process is emotionally driven, for the prospect and the salesperson. An ineffective salesperson reacts to the prospect, which causes the prospect to react, and they end up causing each other to react, thus beginning the cycle of sales failure.

The salesperson needs to be a professional at inspiring the prospect to buy their product or service. This is going to cause a positive reaction in the prospect.

What causes confidence in the salesperson is *knowing* they can save the prospect money, *knowing* they can save the prospect time, and *knowing* their product or service is going to exceed the prospect's expectations.

Confidence would also be having the patience to gain that understanding *without overwhelming the prospect with education.* In other words, stick to the sales process and be confident enough to know that you're going to get to the point where you can present exactly what the customer needs and then transition to the close.

KNOW WHY PROSPECTS RESIST THE SALES PROCESS

Overcoming Resistance

Another aspect of confidence is the ability to overcome sales resistance rapidly and easily.

A fundamental flaw in sales training is that it does not teach salespeople how to identify, isolate, and overcome their prospect's sales resistance. Instead, their training (or lack of it) concentrates on pushing product or service features and benefits. Today's prospects are tired of hearing the same old sales message.

The result of not overcoming resistance is that salespeople don't establish real communication with the prospect. They don't gain enough trust that the prospect talks about their challenges, what they're running into, why they need this product, and why they haven't gotten it yet. Salespeople instead engage in social chit-chat, "Hi, how are you? Nice day! Love your dress!" then launch right into their product's features.

What they're trying to do is overwhelm the prospect with features and benefits instead of addressing their actual needs. Operating in this way, the salesperson will sell to the 2 out of 10 prospects who are going to buy anyway. But that isn't any kind of success level, is it? It's also not profitable at all, as discussed earlier.

**Closing with confidence
8 out of 10 closed**

compared to

**Closing with NO confidence
2 out of 10 closed**

Experience Includes Following the Sales Process

It's true: experience builds confidence. If you follow the sales process and continuously improve these core abilities while you are taking care of the next 10 customers, would that experience be valuable? Would you improve? For sure! By the time you took care of 20, 30, and 40 customers the right way, your life would certainly change! You would be on your way to becoming a top 20% salesperson!

However, if you fail to use the sales process and improve the core abilities, you will fail to improve. Thus breeding a lack of confidence. You can handle 10, 20, even 100 customers the wrong way, which is a *lot* of experience without improvement, continuously failing, and ending up with a low closing rate. Many salespeople "burn out" and leave the job because of this experience.

Experience only builds confidence if you are following the standard process and continually working to improve. By the time you take care of 100 customers, you will be in a much higher condition.

In the end, it is confidence that allows you to penetrate the wall of sales resistance and build trust.

CORE ABILITY #6 - COMPETENCE

COMPETENCE IS IRRESISTIBLE FOR YOUR PROSPECT

Thanks to the internet, buyers today are far more educated than in times past. Due to the deterioration of communication and sales skills, eight out of ten buying experiences are poor. So, nowadays, buyers are far more educated and have far more bad experiences.

It's a rare experience when prospects encounter a competent salesperson who is really educated and who actually follows the sales process—buyers will be immediately attracted to it. An uneducated salesperson is their own worst enemy.

PRESENTING UNDENIABLE EVIDENCE IS HARD TO RESIST

Competence is a vital missing ingredient. You need to be able to make the case for your product or service, show that it exceeds prospect expectations, and inspire prospects to take action to obtain your product or service.

Part of being competent is to effectively show how your product or service is far better than your competitor's. Between the marketing-sales relationship and company strategy, you should always be several steps ahead of the competition.

If your competition is happy being number two, you're doing well at being competent as a company and as a sales team.

If you cannot make the case for your product or service and effectively destroy the competition, you inevitably lose.

Competence would include salespeople providing the Marketing Team with the information they need to create better marketing materials, including sales collateral. This would include the reasons customers buy and the reasons they don't. Your Marketing Team should truly understand what the Sales Team is running into—what objections—so that Marketing can provide sales materials that can handle those objections; collateral salespeople can use.

MAKING THE CASE—MARKETING COLLATERAL FOR THE SALES PROCESS

A very important part of a salesperson making their case is the use of *marketing collateral*. Marketing collateral is any media, print or digital, that makes a strong case for your product or service.

Sales and Marketing collateral leaves no doubt that your product or service is the very best, while planting doubt in the mind of your prospect about your competition.

If you receive a hard-copy piece such as a brochure, you tend to look it over. If you're just receiving an email or see a social media comment or post, there are so many there that they're easy to ignore.

Every day, juries make crucial decisions based on 2 primary factors:

1) the evidence presented, and
2) the emotional impact the lawyer can elicit from the jury.

The evidence presented must leave no doubt that your product exceeds the prospect's expectations, must put doubt in the prospect's mind about your competitor and must create the needed emotional impact to close the deal.

WE BELIEVE WHAT IS SHOWN IN PICTURES AND WRITING

In today's world, people need images, graphics, and messages that jump right out at them, resonate and communicate to them. The images and information they see will greatly assist them in making decisions. This is marketing collateral.

The collateral should be designed like a story, told along the lines of the company's sales process. Prior to the collateral being designed and written, the company should figure out the best possible way to communicate, educate, and strike

at the "pain points" of their prospects. The materials should be designed to guide the prospects to a full understanding of what they can do for the prospect. At the end of the story, the prospect should realize that there is no way they could live without that product or service.

These materials should also be designed to help the *salesperson guide* the prospect through the sales process, step-by-step, in the correct sequence and ideal way.

Competence comes from the fact that the salesperson isn't skipping all over the place, forgetting to say things, or not taking the prospect through every step of the sales process.

The collateral materials can also give the company itself confidence that salespeople will have guidance in what they're discussing with prospects and properly represent the products and services, relating them to the specific needs and wants of every prospect. It is more than just a brochure. Marketing collateral is created specifically to help you, the salesperson, effectively guide your prospect through the sales process resulting in a close. For more information on developing marketing collateral, please feel free to contact SELLability.

MARKETING AND SALES MUST BE A VERY CLOSE TEAM

In our research, we found that marketing and sales teams just don't work together, when in fact it should be the closest relationship within the organization. In order for the marketing team to be able to say that they're effective, the sales team has to sell. Marketing must understand sales, and sales relies on marketing for more qualified leads and prospects.

The goal of marketing collateral is to have the prospect's fear, worry, and doubt replaced by trust, confidence, and a renewed level of interest.

CORE ABILITY #7 - CLOSING

WHAT IS CLOSING ABILITY?

We all know closing the deal is paramount to achieving your goals. Unfortunately, not too many know that the close is not a magic formula or a technique designed to beat a prospect into submission, or twist an unwilling arm, but rather the culmination of all the successful actions prior to this final step.

Closing is an art, a learned ability. Closing is where real salesmanship and ultimate success and profitability happen. It's also simple. The ability to close really comes from being a true professional at the beginning parts of the sales process.

Closing is really the shortest step in the sales process. It is a natural end to doing all the prior work:

a. Becoming a valuable and trusted source of information for your target market.

b. Effectively marketing to your target public.

c. Researching and developing relationships with your target public.

d. Creating an unbreakable trust through real communication.

e. Genuinely caring and focusing on creating lifelong relations with your customers.

f. Obtaining a full understanding of their needs, wants, problems, goals, and dreams.

g. Guiding the customer through the Qualifying process resulting in a clear understanding of why they should buy from their own point of view.

h. Developing a strong desire and care to help your customer through any barriers to purchase your product throughout the process.

i. Ensuring your customers fully understand your products and services and are inspired to take the necessary actions to buy them.

At this point, they're in agreement and the salesperson just transitions to the close.

SOURCE OF CLOSING FAILURES

As mentioned several times throughout this book (for very good reason), the failure to close stems from the failure to complete earlier steps of the sales process.

Salespeople skip through the sales process and as they jump into the close they face the "price obstacle." Since they didn't build value in the earlier stages, now it's all about lowering prices.

If you haven't built the foundation at the beginning of the sales process, the sale will fall apart by the time you reach the Education step.

Remember, the beginning of the sales process is the foundation that will solidly allow you to transition to the rest of the sales process.

Ineffective sales training emphasizes closing techniques; but, how do you close a door that was never opened?

The emphasis here is building value from the very start. Honestly, 95 percent of the work comes before the close. You should walk into that close with the customer pulling you over that closing line saying, "Please take my money!"

How Do You Close A Door That Was Never Open?

Both of us have had people tell us, earlier in the sales process, "Okay, I'm done. I'm closed!" We'll go ahead and take the money, but we'll always finish the remaining steps of the sales process, and often obtain even more business in the process. Finishing the process allows you to capture all the needed information.

Again (and it can't be stated too many times) closing is *never* the issue. The issue is whether all the previous steps of the sales process are successfully and fully completed.

BUILDING VALUE PRIOR TO CLOSING IS VITAL

Building value includes fully completing all steps prior to the Education step. If you have done each of the steps leading up to Education, the value should exceed the prospect's expectations and inspire them to take action (the end result of Education). If you fail to build this value prior to getting to Agreement or Closing, you are now stuck handling objections at the end and you are likely to be stressed or feel stuck.

Why? You probably missed the fact that the prospect was not telling you everything they were thinking. This caused you to miss something. You were unable to ask the right questions to thoroughly understand their existing situation. It is also likely that you were unable to thoroughly understand their goals and dreams.

Remember, what you are selling is the difference between where they are now and where they want to be. You need to support where they want to be and increase that difference even more as you present the value of your product or service. This must be a *big difference*! If not, the gap is too small and you will often be stuck at the Agreement or Close steps.

Before you close them on their dream scenario, you must thoroughly understand their existing situation so you can see the gap between where they are now and where they're going to be after they obtain your product or service. The bigger that gap is, the easier it is to close. You're closing them on the dream, but the gap between where they are today and where they're going to be needs to be big enough that the customer transitions easily to the close. That's what you're doing with the sales process, and that's what you're doing at the close.

THE REWARD FOR TRULY UNDERSTANDING CLOSING

With a clear understanding of how to build value for their product or service, top salespeople close deals effortlessly at *higher margins*.

The end result at closing is a salesperson who is totally certain, and a prospect who is certain they're making the right decision.

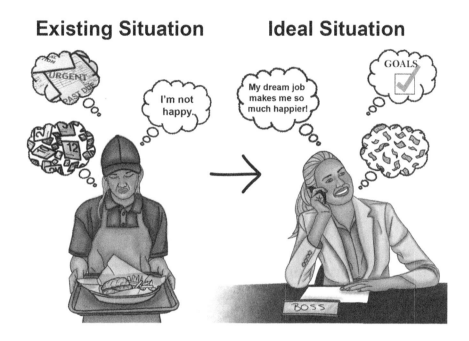

CORE ABILITY #8 - CUSTOMER RELATIONSHIP

SELLING IS AN EXCHANGE WHERE BOTH PARTIES WIN

Always remember: *selling is an exchange where both parties win.* Therefore, it's not enough to just make the sale and move on.

As covered in the chapter on the sales process, establishing a customer relationship involves the delivery of your product or service. Delivery is crucial. This is also where the buying cycle begins all over again, after all, the better the exchange, the more your new client will make the decision to not only retain your services and become a lifelong customer but feel you are trustworthy enough to refer you to others.

PROSPERITY COMES WITH THREE FLOWS OF SALES LEADS AND PROSPECTS INTO YOUR BUSINESS

There are three flows of potential prospects that should be coming into your company. You should track them.

1. Marketing leads and reaches: prospects flowing in directly from marketing actions
2. Happy customers continuing to buy more products and services
3. Referrals from happy customers

If you have all 3 of these flows working, you're not going to have a scarcity of prospects. If you're missing one of these three, you run the risk of scarcity, which places more pressure on your sales process. If there's pressure on your sales process, you're going to make mistakes.

SPLITTING THE FOCUS OF YOUR SALESPEOPLE CAN KILL YOUR EXPANSION

We have seen many companies put salespeople or account representatives in charge of selling to both new customers and reselling to existing customers. This is especially prevalent in small businesses and start-ups. As the company starts to grow and experience expansion, the available attention salespeople tend to have will become less as they get spread thinner and thinner.

You can see this statistically in that one or the other will suffer (sales to new customers vs. repeat sales to existing customers). Salespeople tend to go towards potential sales that can be closed easily, especially because this affects their commissions. As a result, sometimes the sales to existing customers will go up and down and sometimes the sales to new customers will go up and down. We call this the roller-coaster of sales, which is never fun. In this scenario, neither will reach their full potential.

By building teams sperate teams and focusing your sales-people on one or the other, both types of sales can expand.

As you will see in the customer journey in the next few pages, new business is driven into the company and as those customers journey through the sales and delivery process, the account manager takes over to ensure they are continuously serviced and winning which causes them to buy again and refer others to buy.

In this way, both new and existing customers grow, and the business expands. By having salespeople handling both new and existing customers and splitting their attention between them, companies tend to experience ups and downs and pressure on revenue.

The Customer Development Journey

Illustrating the 3 flows of Potential Income

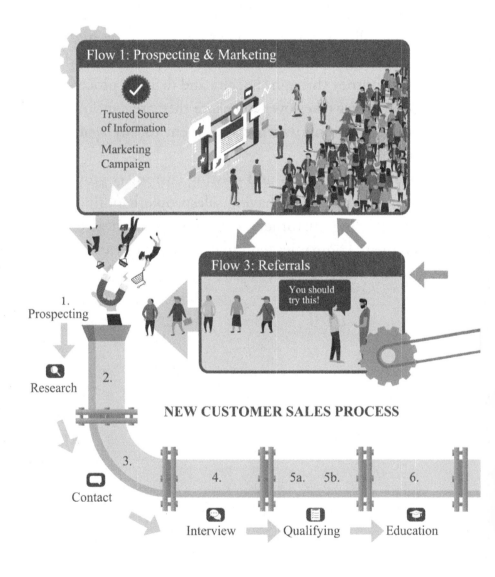

This graphic illustrates the customer development journey. The process starts with prospecting and marketing (illustrated as Flow 1). After you have become a trusted source of information, you can then start marketing campaigns to attract leads. Leads then flow into the New Customer Sales Process (illustrated below-left as the first pipeline). At the end of the new customer sales process you must provide stellar delivery. Flow 2 and Flow 3 are rewards you get for providing a stellar delivery of products and services. They are also extremely low cost in comparison to flow 1. For more information on each of the sections in this illustration, refer to the next two pages for more detailed information.

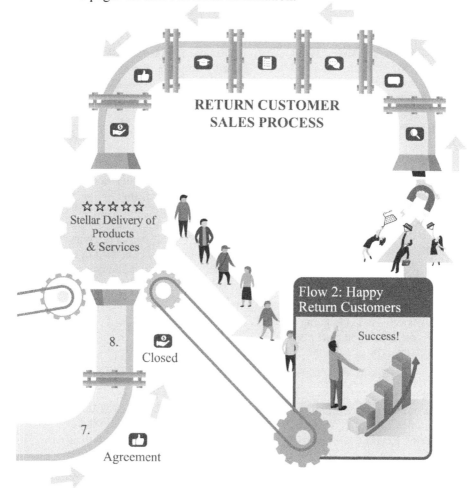

Flow 1.

PROSPECTING RESULT
Focus on being a "Trusted Source of Information".
You've developed a huge database of potential prospects, of the public that will buy your products or services. You have provided the public with valuable free content, keeping them actively in communication with your company, resulting in your company being considered a valuable source of information AND a company the prospects can TRUST!
This can be done through articles, information library, publications, video, social media, radioWith that in place, you can now research, and then contact those public and develop them into prospects who will smoothly go into communication at the contact step and move through the sales process.

MARKETING CAMPAIGN
A marketing campaign can now be effective to the prospects who already trust you.

1. PROSPECTING
Result:
Abundance of qualified prospects responding and reaching your products and services.

2. RESEARCH
Result:
You've cared enough to establish a foundation of information which is going to allow the Contact and Interview step to go more smoothly. This is going to allow you to develop trust much more efficiently.

3. CONTACT
Result:
Focus on manners & granting importance.
Lowering Resistance - Hope of Trust

You've established enough trust that your prospect is willing to disclose to you what they are truly thinking. Achieving this will then lead to a successful Qualifying step.

4. INTERVIEW
Result:
Focus on developing trust
Listening, truly understanding, being interested, and acknowledging your prospect.

You've established enough trust that your prospect is willing to disclose to you what they are truly thinking. Achieving this will then lead to a successful Qualifying step.

5a. QUALIFYING
Result:
Qualifying result for salespeople in the top 20 percent:
A) You know all the reasons why the prospect should buy, from the prospect's point of view.
B) Ideally, you also know, as part of that, how to save the customer money, and save them

time. How to make them money, what problems you're solving for them, and how you're supporting their goals.

C) You also know how long they've had their problems, how long they've had these goals and dreams, and how much money and time they have wasted on similar products and services that didn't get them the result.

D) You've decided if you're willing to have a lifelong relationship with that prospect.

5b. QUALIFYING FOCUSED ON LOGISTICS

We found that the Qualifying result from salespeople in the lower percentage (the remaining 80 percent of salespeople) basically focused on logistics:

E) What is the prospect's buying process?

F) Does the prospect have the budget?

These last two are also important but secondary to A-D to the left. Only worrying about logistics is a major reason salespeople don't close.

6. EDUCATION

Result:
The customer knows that your product or service will exceed their expectations, and the customer is inspired to take action to obtain the product or service.

7. AGREEMENT

Result:
During or at the end of the Agreement step, the customer has firmly decided to buy and has voiced that decision.

8. CLOSED

Motivation tied to this Result!:
The result of the closing step is the successful transition of the prospect from the salesperson to the delivery team. This frees up the salesperson to completely focus on the sales process with another customer. Attention is no longer tied up in the worry of whether or not the previous customer will be taken care of.

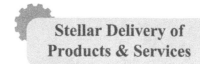

Stellar Delivery of Products & Services

Flow 2.

RETURN CUSTOMERS

Because the delivery exceeds customer expectations, they are now inspired to buy again.

Flow 3.

REFERRALS

Because the delivery exceeds customer expectations, they are now inspired to take action referring their friends and colleagues.

Flow 2 and Flow 3 are rewards you get for providing a stellar delivery of products and services.

POOR DELIVERY=

NO REFERRALS OR RETURNING CUSTOMERS

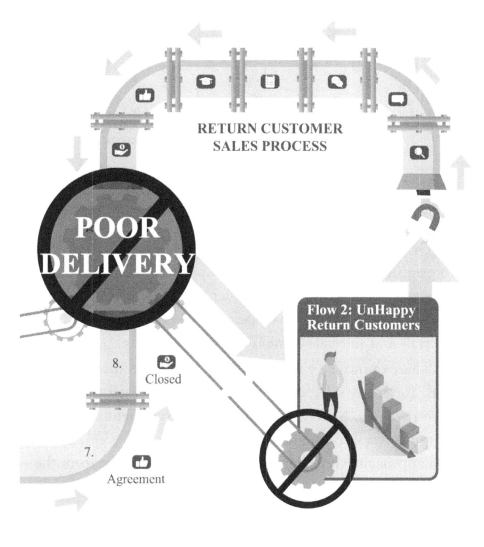

POOR DELIVERY =
NO REFERRALS OR RETURNING CUSTOMERS
= LOST INCOME FROM 2 SOURCES
= UNNECESSARY MARKETING & SALES PRESSURE!

WHEN THERE IS A SCARCITY OF PROSPECTS, A LOT OF PRESSURE IS ON THE SALESPERSON TO SKIP STEPS AND JUST CLOSE. THIS CONTRIBUTES TO THE 80/20 PROBLEM.

On the referral angle, referrals are another primary reason to establish a fantastic relationship with your new client after the close. Too few happy clients lead to too few referral opportunities. The great salesperson makes a great living from referrals and referrals come from stellar delivery.

There cannot be enough said about the customer relationship. Too many salespeople move on once they get that close. If you want to build a lifelong, ever-after affluent company, you must establish a great relationship with all your clients. You approach every client as a lifelong relationship from the beginning.

The successful salesperson never misses an opportunity to win referrals at the right time. Their current and past clients are loyal to a fault and help drive new business.

MANAGING BY STATISTICS/ KPI'S

Note on statistics: managing statistics is vital for your business and is vital for all salespeople. Each week, track how many prospects you receive from:

1. Marketing
2. Referrals and
3. Repeat business

You must track and graph all three. It has been said that you can manage by hope, manage by feelings, or manage by statistics. SELLability strongly recommends the 3rd (statistics).

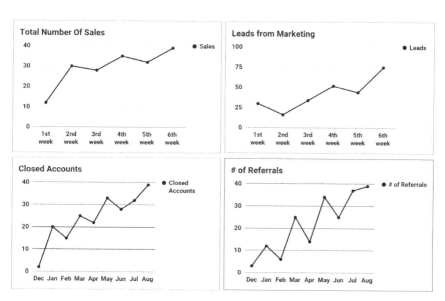

Now you know the core abilities you need to develop in order to master the sales process! These are the abilities the top 20% of salespeople continuously improve and maintain throughout their careers. Mastering these skills is vital to solving the 80/20 problem.

INTERLUDE

Remember the *Rule of 8* from chapter 3? These next chapters are a considerable expansion of the *Rule of 8*, which is a vital foundation needed to be ready to qualify a prospect.

THE RULE OF 8

1. The vital necessity of using good manners and etiquette.

   Et-i-quette Noun \ 'e-ti-kət, - ket\: the rules indicating the proper and polite way to behave (including appearance)

2. Grant importance: show respect, awareness of their position and/or experience.

   Note: This step does not always have to be verbal. Feel free to contact SELLability (SELLability.com) for more information.

3. Establish agreement: what can you both agree on?

4. Discover interest: what motivated them to call, to take your call, or to visit with you?

5. Address prior prospect experience: any prior experience(s) with this product or service, or a product or service similar to yours?

6. Envision the future: what are their future expectations in regard to this product or service?

7. Get an up-front agreement: if I can show how this product or service would save you time and/or money and solve _____ problem, would you be willing to move forward?

8. Continue to QUALIFY as you begin to PRESENT.

Qualifying is, of course, the make-break point of a sale. It's the hump that you either get over and do extremely well, or you don't, and you move on to another opportunity. It should be very clear at the end of qualifying if the sale is going to close or not. If you, as the salesperson, have not decided that the prospect will buy at that point, it is likely that the qualifying step is not completed. Either the prospect is qualified and you have fully decided the sale will close, or the prospect is not qualified.

As we covered earlier, you won't make it through the Qualifying step unless your prospect is willing to tell you everything you need to know to qualify them. And *that* won't happen unless they trust you. Trust is built through all of the steps prior to qualifying. If those steps are thoroughly done, qualifying will occur and the sale will close.

4

MANNERS AND ETIQUETTE

B efore we start, let's define some words.

etiquette [ˈɛtɪˌkɛt ˌɛtɪˈkɛt] *n*
1. (Sociology) the customs or rules governing behavior regarded as correct or acceptable in social or official life.
2. (Sociology) a conventional but unwritten code of practice followed by members of any of certain professions or groups.
Collins English Dictionary – Complete and Unabridged
© HarperCollins Publishers 1991, 1994, 1998, 2000, 2003
According to Wikipedia, "**Etiquette** is a code of behavior that delineates expectations for social behavior according to contemporary conventional norms within a society, social class, or group."

Now, let's look at a good definition of manners from a book entitled *Today's Etiquette,* written by Lillian Eichler and published in 1941 by Doubleday Doran: "Good manners are not only indispensable in society, but they have a very practical value in the business world."

Manners and etiquette play a large role in business, and especially in sales. For example, whether in a sales or a social situation, talking too much would not be considered good manners. But according to a worldwide survey conducted by SELLability, this offense is committed by salespeople all the time.

Good manners and communication skills work hand-in-hand for salespeople and must be part of a salesperson's skill set.

Etiquette When Greeting Your Prospect

Hi, Nice to meet you! Welcome to my office.

Oh hey, yeah hold on a sec.

Good **Bad**

GRANTING IMPORTANCE TO OTHERS

Manners begin with granting importance to people, their ideas, and their communication. Granting importance is so vital that we've dedicated an entire chapter to it, which we'll get to shortly. But it bears mentioning with specific reference to manners.

Have you ever met someone who seemed convinced they knew everything, and failed to show any interest in you or your ideas? How did this make you feel?

Such conduct is highly dangerous in sales. Salespeople who assume they "know it all already" and fail to grant importance to prospective clients will not succeed. In fact, they cannot help but fail because they won't see or hear what the prospect is communicating. Such salespeople tend to leave a meeting thinking that the prospect will call them just like the prospect probably said they would but the prospect never does.

CAUSE OF PROSPECTS NOT RETURNING CALLS

Guess what? *This is the major cause of a prospect or client not returning your calls after the first contact by phone or meeting in person.* If you or your sales team have difficulty consistently getting a prospective client back into communication after an initial meeting, the cause is likely a lack of truly paying attention to, hearing, and understanding the prospective client.

As a test or exercise, try this after a meeting: ask yourself what you learned about that prospective client. If you truly were paying attention and listening, there will be a full profile of the prospective client, their ideas, and a good understanding of how they feel and what they are interested in, right there in the front of your mind. You can conduct the same test on other salespeople or members of your sales team. Use this as an opportunity to improve this skill.

Granting importance is the first step in succeeding as a salesperson. Your prospective client needs to feel that they are important to you, important enough that they'll start feeling comfortable and will trust you.

AGENDAS OR SCRIPTED OPENINGS ARE BAD MANNERS IN AN INITIAL MEETING

Outside of sales, when you meet someone for the first time, do you normally have a pre-planned focus to get that person to do something for you? Are you working from an agenda, or following a script? Probably not. So, why would you do this as a salesperson?

Something else you would never do in a social situation outside of sales: "Hi, my name is _____ and I would like to go to dinner with you tomorrow night. I already know you will like me very much because many other people like me and I can see already that you are a nice person who would like to go to dinner with me."

This would never work as your opening statement, would it? Why do this same thing as a salesperson when meeting your client for the first time? "Hi my name is _____ and I would like you to buy my product or service. I already know that you will like my product because many other people like my product and I can see already that you are a nice person who likes good products and services like mine."

Okay, these are great examples of bad manners in an initial meeting. Let's take a look at what *good* manners would look like when meeting someone for the first time. Let's say a good friend of yours stopped by your home and brought a guest with them. What would you do?

You would probably introduce yourself, offer them a refreshment, and make sure they were comfortable. Next, you might find out how they know your friend, what they do for a living, and discover what their interests are. Additionally, you would listen to what this person was saying and try to understand their point of view. You would even ask more questions to clarify and understand them better.

You would do all of this without expectations or demands on them, without any agenda in mind other than really understanding their point of view.

These are good manners in life and this is exactly how you should behave when you meet your client for the first time.

You would also seek to be yourself in social situations, wouldn't you? It's the same in sales. You wouldn't suddenly become "Super Salesperson" or "Sales Samurai" when meeting a client. When people like you, they like *you*, not "you being someone else." People can tell the difference between a person who is genuine, trustworthy, and truly caring, and a person who is fake and only trying to sell.

MANNERS IN A DIGITAL WORLD

Since we live in such an electronic and mobile society, a chapter on manners wouldn't be complete without a word on cell phone manners.

Have you ever tried to have a conversation with someone who is constantly texting on their phone or another device? It's frustrating and very bad manners. Somehow, such behavior has become acceptable in business. During a sales meeting, half the team is on their phones or devices texting. People cannot seem to be detached from their phones or tablets long enough to have their full attention on a meeting or conversation.

It is extremely poor manners to do this in a meeting with a prospect or client. Doing so conveys an instant impression that you do not care enough about that client. You'll have enough to deal with in getting through that prospect's sales

resistance, don't add to it by constantly paying attention to your phone or device. Even if it is on vibrate, the prospect can hear the vibration.

Your sales team meetings will be more efficient and productive if you have a policy to turn off devices during the meeting. And a note to husbands and wives: it's a good practice to have dinner with your cell phones off. More quality time together!

REFERRALS

As any top sales rep will tell you, referrals are the best leads you can get. Put simply, obtaining referrals comes from taking care of your clients well, using good manners and communication skills with them, and ensuring your company delivers a great product or service. When all of these factors are present, asking for referrals can usually be done with great results.

REFERRALS VS NAMES

There is a common misunderstanding between a referral and just a name. The key difference between the two is that a referral comes with an introduction. This introduction provided by your customer to their friend or colleague opens the door to creating the relationship and easily transitioning to your standard sales process. Without the introduction, you just have a name, this is a BIG difference. Make sure that your team defines a referral in this way. This one change makes referrals way more valuable and will result in higher closing rates!

Once you get a referral, manners come into play as well. A referral is usually a colleague or friend of your client, and you are now entrusted by your client to handle their friend or colleague in a manner that validates the fact that they recommended you and your company.

8 MAJOR POINTS OF MANNERS AND ETIQUETTE TO REMEMBER WHEN TAKING CARE OF A CLIENT REFERRAL

1. Do your homework.

When you first get the referral, find out all you can about them—their company, their interests, their history, how your client knows them, and anything else you feel would help.

Ask your client why they think yours would be a good company and what you could best provide for their referral. Then, conduct further research about the referral and their company through online searches and any other mutual colleagues who know this company or referral.

You should have a very good understanding of this referral before you ever make contact. This shows you paid attention to the information from your client and care for the referral they have given you. It also goes a long way toward a great relationship with your new referral when you first make contact.

2. Contact the referral immediately.

Once your homework is complete, contact the referral. Countless times, we have been told by companies we were consulting, "we don't have enough prospects." The first thing we do is look for referrals that were never called. It is very bad manners not to contact your referrals immediately and will shut down the number of referrals you receive.

3. Use good manners when making contact with the referral.

Remember that in the eyes of the referral you not only represent yourself and your company but your client and *their* company as well. That's a lot of reputations you're having to be responsible for! Good manners must be used at all times.

4. Establish trust and solid communication with the referral before moving to the sales appointment.

The first step in taking care of a referral is to establish solid communication and trust with them. Not only does this make the referral feel cared for, but it also validates the client for the referral they have given you. Ensure this step is accomplished *before* getting into a discussion about your products or services.

5. Keep your client regularly informed about the progress with the referral they have given you.

It is important to the client that the referral is well taken care of; so, keep the client informed of progress. They want to know that it is going well and are normally willing to help if there are problems such as having trouble making contact. The client is perfectly able to resolve this by making a personal introduction.

6. Acknowledge your client for giving you the referral.

None of us appreciate helping a colleague and then receiving no acknowledgment for having done so. At the very least, a "thank you" is very important and goes a long way toward obtaining additional referrals in the future.

If you haven't done so, you should develop a regular referrals program in your company that continuously takes care to get referrals and acknowledges the clients who provide them. This machine can be a continuous generation system so that there is never a shortage of referrals.

7. Ask for additional referrals from your client.

Having done all the work to ensure the referral is well taken care of, and having kept the client informed, you are in a position to ask for additional referrals from the same client. This is not only appropriate but expected and welcomed—*if* you have taken care of the first referral very well!

8. Take care of the new client you now have, ask for referrals, and start the process again.

Now that you have taken care of the referral well and have established them as a new client, ask for referrals from *them*. The process starts over with step 1, above.

MANNERS WHILE TRAVELING

Many salespeople travel a great deal. We've both traveled our entire lives. Here we share some of our experience in regards to the importance of manners while traveling. Just to qualify ourselves, we have traveled to 25 countries, logged more than 300,000 miles by plane, and have traveled many additional miles by train, taxi, and car and this is just during the last 12 months!

BE COURTEOUS AND SIMPLY HELP YOUR FELLOW TRAVELERS

There is already enough stress and confusion in traveling. If each of us takes a little more responsibility for our fellows, we may add some calm and happiness to the experience for all. Simple examples include being courteous in all communications—for example, when waiting in line, make a nice comment about someone or ask them where they are traveling to.

SET THE EXAMPLE

Most travelers are not used to the modern travel experience—and yes, we would call it an experience. From the time you leave home, through the check-in line, to the security line, to the line at the gate, to the line to get on the plane, there are delays, inconveniences, and annoyances.

Those of us who travel are used to the rules and barriers of this game and have successful methods of reducing delays and stresses. Recognize that most people around you when you travel are not "professional travelers" and don't have such methods. You are therefore surrounded by the additional stress and confusion that every new traveler is now going through.

Be the calming professional who balances the stress and sets the example. You will see that your influence is contagiously calming, which is also very important for airport and airline personnel. We have earned much respect and even made new friends and clients just by setting that example.

In summary, good etiquette and manners are a critical part of salesmanship and should be part of your continuous improvement system for yourself and your sales team. The Rule of 8 was developed because we found most lost sales are lost early in the sales process before the Educate step. These 8 skills are a major contributor to the 80/20 gap. Lack of these 8 key skills results in low closing rates.

Now, let's expand the subject of manners into an embracive topic – granting importance and respect.

5

GRANTING IMPORTANCE AND RESPECT TO YOUR PROSPECT

B efore we go any further, let's once again define some words.

Grant—To give or accord: *to grant permission*

Importance—Social status; standing; esteem: *a man of importance*

Respect—The state of being honored or esteemed

Collins English Dictionary – Complete and Unabridged © HarperCollins Publishers 1991, 1994, 1998, 2000, 2003

SETTING THE TONE

You're the one, believe it or not, who sets the tone for your meetings. When you first meet someone and in subsequent meetings greet them with happiness and warmth. Make them feel welcome and important. We all love this. When we go to someone else's home or business and we immediately feel welcome, we can relax.

Making someone feel welcome can be as simple as truly being happy to see them, having prepared a comfortable place for them to sit down, and offering a drink or snack. Your first step is to make the person feel like they belong there. In sales, this helps to immediately reduce the resistance to the sales process.

You should always prepare the meeting space in advance. In fact, a good rule of thumb is to have a meeting space always

prepared, so that even if someone comes in unexpectedly, there is coffee, tea, fruit, and snacks already there or can be prepared in 5-10 minutes.

Conversely, when meeting someone at their office or home, if offered a drink, accept it. Why? Because it is an attempt by the prospect to make you feel more comfortable. If you refuse it, it can make the prospect feel uncomfortable which won't help your sales process.

PAYING GENUINE ATTENTION TO YOUR PROSPECTS

The foundation of granting importance begins with simply paying attention to the prospect, understanding their interests, and truly caring about their thoughts. In fact, the importance of this cannot be underestimated: *Giving the prospect your full attention from initial contact is vital to the success of the rest of the sales process, including being able to close the sale.*

Can you think of a friend or colleague whom you like to go to or lean on when you have a problem or are just trying to work something out? Normally this person is a very good listener. They do not necessarily solve your problems for you, but they listen well and then give you a chance to work out a solution. You love them for this. This is the characteristic that, when you adopt it as a salesperson, will have prospects calling you back consistently just because you care enough to pay attention and listen to them.

FOCUS WITHOUT INTERRUPTING

Have you had it happen that a prospect is trying to tell you a story or something about themselves or their company, and you are reminded of a story you know or something you need to tell them? You either cut them off to tell them what you are thinking so you do not forget or, worse, you stop paying attention and cannot wait until the prospect is done so that you can tell them what you thought of. This is very bad manners.

We can agree though, that it does happen sometimes. Just like when a friend is telling you a joke and during their joke, you think of a joke you think is even better; you cannot wait until they are done, give them a courtesy laugh and tell them your joke. If you do this on a regular basis, it is hard to keep

friends. Another example is with spouses having to keep the attention and interest with each other focused, or this creates problems as well.

PRACTICE MAKES GOOD HABITS

Practice paying attention to your friend and family communications. Work to really understand them and care enough to let them know what you think and how you can support their ideas. Get a partner to play the role of a prospect and practice letting the prospect tell a story about their company or themselves. Truly pay attention and stay interested and at the end, validate their story or idea by showing that you understood.

KEEPING THE PROSPECT'S ATTENTION

Have you ever had a thought during your presentation that the prospect is no longer paying attention to you? If you have this thought, guess what? They really *are* no longer paying attention to you, otherwise, you would not have this thought.

Once it occurs to you that the prospect is not paying attention to you anymore, where does your attention go? Of course, you are now worried that they are not paying attention, so *you* end up no longer paying attention. Then neither you nor the prospect is paying attention and nothing is getting accomplished in that presentation.

If you do have this thought during your presentation, stop and ask the prospect about it, a simple statement such as, "Just want to make sure you're still with me, okay?" At worst, the prospect will say, "Yes, I'm okay" and be back with you.

Also, remember that your presentation should align with what you discover in the qualifying step. This is why paying attention is so vital, so that your presentation is laser-precise and focuses exactly on the prospect's interests. Doing this will effectively keep your prospects interested throughout your presentation.

FIRST MEETING—FIRST IMPRESSION

Meeting the prospect for the first time (in person or on the phone) creates the critical impression that will either cause the prospect to stay in communication with you or avoid communication with you in the future. It is vital that the impression you create sets you apart from the average salesperson.

KEEP DISTRACTION-FREE

An important factor in making a great first impression is to remove as many distractions from the salesperson's sphere as possible. Ensure that you and your sales team are fully focused on each initial prospect meeting without distractions.

Complete any projects or administration before leaving at the end of the day so that the stress of incomplete tasks does not build up, causing you or your team to constantly be rushed. This condition of stress or overwhelm is easily seen by your prospect, and they may consider that you are too busy to really care for or pay attention to their needs.

GOOD IMPRESSIONS ARE A BOOST TO THE QUALIFYING PROCESS

Creating a positive initial impression allows the qualifying process to be more successful.

Qualifying was defined earlier, in the Sales Process chapter. In qualifying, the prospect must be willing to *tell you* all about their needs, wants, timing, budget, and purchase process, as well as why they should buy your product or service, from *their* viewpoint. But, if you are not paying attention and do a poor job creating that good first impression, your prospect will not give you the data you need to qualify. If you *do* pay attention and create a great initial impression, the prospect is more willing to tell you everything they know and are thinking about.

If you are unable to obtain the information needed for qualifying, or if the prospect is unwilling to provide it to you, you have missed something in the initial impression. You must continue to work on this point until you gain the trust and willingness of the prospect to provide you the information. If you are not paying close attention and maintaining interest during the qualifying process, you are likely to miss vital information you need to complete this step.

Granting importance and respect ties directly into establishing agreement, and vice versa, which of course leads directly to our next topic.

8 Ways To Make A Bad Impression.

6

ESTABLISHING AGREEMENT

The subject of communication was covered thoroughly in Chapter 2. Communication skills are extremely important and must be utilized throughout the sales process. Here, we will focus on its importance in establishing agreement. Without communication, agreement won't occur.

In actuality, you're establishing agreement during the entire sales process. It begins with communication itself. Then, you're going into manners and etiquette and then into granting importance, which we also covered in previous chapters. If you've done these things well, your prospect will certainly be in agreement with you.

AGREEMENT BUILDS TRUST

You will certainly need agreement as you get close to the qualifying step. Agreement builds trust, which is actually what you're doing, step by step. We tend to trust people with whom we agree.

DISAGREEMENT LEADS TO MISTRUST

In contrast, disagreement leads to mistrust. We can look at the state of politics in the world and see this in action—there is a huge amount of disagreement; hence, a huge amount of mistrust.

DISAGREEMENT IS UNCOMFORTABLE

When you meet someone for the first time, what are you trying to naturally accomplish? Of course, you are working to establish agreement.

That first moment can be awkward, like when you met your spouse, boss, or any friend for the first time. We are trying to fit in, be liked, and just find a way to get comfortable in a potentially uncomfortable first meeting. We do this naturally by searching out anything we can talk about that is agreeable. The conversation can start with the weather, clothing, cultural origin, sports, or anything else which can be agreed upon. We tend to stay away from anything controversial to avoid offending the other person.

BE YOURSELF

It is no different when you meet your prospect for the first time. As we've been doing throughout this book, we want to emphasize again that people like you for being yourself, not for trying to be something or someone you are not. We are constantly amazed at some of the sales professionals who feel they must put on their "super salesperson suit" and become someone else in order to sell.

What you *must* create at this point is *trust*. Who will trust you if you're trying to be someone else? Be yourself and find *real* points of agreement.

AGREEMENT LEADS TO TRUST AND FURTHER COMMUNICATION

In a sales situation, this is a vital step because we need the prospect to be willing to talk to us. If there is no (or very little) agreement established, the prospect will not communicate very much because they will not trust us. Do you normally trust someone you disagree with? Do you like someone you disagree with? Do you trust someone you don't like? It all works together and is a vital foundation for your success in the rest of the sales process.

Note that in the earlier steps of the sales process, especially the Contact and Interview step, you will discover numerous subjects and items your prospect can agree with. It's very important that you keep track of these. Take note.

YOUR PROSPECT CANNOT ARGUE
WITH THEIR OWN AGREEMENTS

Your prospect cannot argue with things they themselves agree with. That is why agreement and tracking it throughout the sales process is so important.

Establishing agreement will help you to break through what your prospect isn't telling you about—their past experience. Prospects rarely buy products or services they disagree with. This starts with agreement with their salesperson. Another key skill of the top 20% of salespeople. They rapidly create agreement with their prospects and expand those agreements throughout the sales process. The prospect is then willing to share more of their true thoughts and past experiences.

And that's where we're going next.

7

WHAT YOUR PROSPECT ISN'T TELLING YOU: THEIR PAST EXPERIENCE

W hen you've applied the techniques of the previous chapters with your prospect, it is much easier to accurately determine their interest in your product or service. If you try to skip any steps, this becomes more difficult.

PROSPECT'S VIEWPOINT

We mentioned this earlier, but it is important enough to be covered again: you need to find what the prospect is interested in *from their point of view*, not yours as the salesperson. You may come up with reasons the prospect should buy your product or service; such reasons might include but are not limited to, quality, value, aesthetics, experience, features, or discounts. The thing is, *you may be right about all of them!* But whose point of view is this? *Yours!* It is vital that you find out why the *prospect* should buy, from *their* point of view.

Many times the prospect does not have it all worked out for themselves yet and then it is the job of the salesperson to help them do so. You do this by guiding the prospect to look for themselves at the reasons they decided they needed this product or service. This means not only asking questions, but asking the *right* questions. As you do this and patiently listen, the prospect is able to work through any uncertainty for themselves. Similar to you or I being able to "talk through a problem", with a person we trust, and by doing this we come up with solutions.

CHANGING A VIEWPOINT

You will never get someone else to change their viewpoint unless you first understand what their point of view is and why they feel that way. This takes patience and is a vital skill the top 20% of salespeople apply in all aspects of their lives. An example we used earlier is parents trying to convince children to clean their room. Whose room is it? The child's of course. The room is a mess—but from whose point of view? The parent's! For the child, it's just fine. Do we, as parents, ever find out what the child actually thinks about it? What is their point of view? Why do they feel that way?

If you have children, an interesting experiment is to get down on their level. Ask the child to give you a tour of their room, and to tell you all about it. What do they see? What do they like about it? What don't they like about it? What would they change or improve? In the end, you'll fully understand the child's view. And for the child, it might be the first time someone was interested enough to find out what they think. Applying this skill is a life changer.

In fact, if a parent can learn to constantly ask for their kid's viewpoint, and then be patient enough to listen, understand, and acknowledge it, their relationship with their kid is going to remain strong throughout their life. If a parent ever wanted to restore that relationship or strengthen it, that would be a good place to start: just really be interested in what the kid thinks.

It's a similar situation for the prospect, you must genuinely obtain their viewpoint. The prospect's viewpoint is key to eventually showing how your product or service supports what they are trying to achieve.

The prospect cannot argue or disagree with their own viewpoint, can they? They can always argue or disagree with the salesperson's viewpoint. If you really find out why the prospect should buy—from *their* point of view—and then show how your product or service supports that viewpoint, the prospect will have a hard time arguing or giving you objections to buying.

FINDING THAT VIEWPOINT TAKES INTEREST

The key to discovering the prospect's viewpoint is to be truly interested in them. This is a basic key to selling anything. Being interested in people is what will make you successful in sales.

What is the very first question you ask the prospective client? You can start by asking yourself what you want to know about this prospect. The most obvious thing you want to know is what caused the prospect to make contact or have an interest. Was it a marketing or promotion piece? An advertisement? Did a friend refer them to you?

Find out what interested your prospect enough to call. If you are calling on the prospect, find out how much they know about you, your product or service. Same idea. They were interested enough to talk to you, so what do they know?

FOLLOWING IT DOWN, GAINING A FULL UNDERSTANDING

Let's take an example. You learn from the prospect that they called because of a promotion they received or an advertisement they saw. Most salespeople will just go with that answer, but if you are honestly interested, you'll take it further. How about finding out what they liked most about the promotion, or what it was about the promo that caused them to take action and contact you? This gives you additional information about what the prospect is thinking and what they are interested in.

According to statistics cited earlier, the average American is shown over 5,000 messages *per day* through push marketing—radio, TV, social media, email, text, billboards, and others. This comes out to over 35,000 messages per week, over 150,000 messages per month, and more than 1.5 million messages per year! It does grant importance to the prospect given the fact that out of all those messages they received, they reached out to you.

Take your questioning of the prospect even further, building up a high communication level. You may ask "How long have you been thinking about buying a product or service like mine?" which is also an important question you need answered. If your prospect tells you that they have been thinking about it for 6 months, a year, or even more, that's something you're very interested in.

You can also ask a question like "I am curious; why didn't you buy the product or service before now?" Getting this information and being interested in as much detail as possible is very key and will set a good foundation of communication and trust with your prospect. It's also crucial if, later on in the sales process, they give you the age-old stall, "I need to think about it." We'll cover how this works in a bit.

Average Push Marketing Pieces
(Radio, TV, social media, email, text, billboards, etc)
5,000 day, 35,000 a week,150,000 a month, 5 million a year

PRIOR EXPERIENCES GOOD OR BAD

Realistically, what you've established to arrive at this stage of the sales process—and what you've continued to strengthen—is trust. And the real situation with prospects is that they've had prior experiences with sales, some good, some bad. We have established, through years of research and talking to people, that most have had more bad experiences with salespeople than good.

This is another reason the prospect isn't telling you what they're thinking. So, in asking these important questions, part of what you're uncovering is their past experience.

Most salespeople are not willing to take up any bad experience the prospect may have had. But you must! The problem is that bad experience is interfering, preventing that sale from moving forward because the prospect is afraid their current experience will end up like their past experience.

So, the first step is to uncover the bad experience and get them to tell you all about it. There was some pain involved in that experience, and that pain is now being described as a waste of time and money for the prospect.

Get into the details: how long did that experience last? If it was something that they've already bought, how long have they had that product or service? It could be that the prior experience wasn't only that they made a bad purchase, but that they were stuck with it for a lengthy period of time.

Past bad experiences always cost your prospects two things:

1. Time
2. Money

Find out about these things from your prospects to open the door to being able to save them time and money with your product or service.

Of course, prior experiences aren't all bad. If the prospect tells you, "Well, you know, I did have a good experience once," get them to tell you about it. What made it good? What did they like about it? These would all be points to tie into agreement (which, remember, we're strengthening as we go) because that good experience is something they can easily agree with.

At the end of this conversation, you could also ask what they would change or improve about that experience to make it even better. That will bring you more points of agreement.

If you've done your work well and your prospect trusts you, they'll tell you all about these things. Your job is to understand them, acknowledge them, and get them to tell you more until they've literally told you *all* about it.

WHY UNCOVERING PAST EXPERIENCE IS VITAL

The reason this step is so important is that, from the time you first meet the prospect, their prior experiences are preventing them from telling you what they truly think. The problem is, they won't tell you their prior experiences until you've developed trust—which is why you must follow the sales process step by step.

Unless you uncover that prior experience, you're not going to make the sale. The prospect may, during the sales process, be consciously or unconsciously reminded of negative prior experiences. A lot of what happens during the sales process is that we, as buyers, are reminded of mistakes we've made in the past. We certainly don't want to make those mistakes again.

It's the job of the salesperson to really get the prospect to share those prior experiences, and for the salesperson to really understand them. The reason this is so important is that when we get to the Education step of the sales process, we're going to show them a big difference between their prior experiences and what they're going to experience now and into the future.

This again goes back to what we covered in the beginning of this chapter (and elsewhere in this book) about viewpoint, you cannot change a point of view without first really understanding it.

The prospect has never been able to tell someone all about that bad experience, never had someone just listen to them talk about it. If you're the person who stays interested, stays patient, and fully listens to the whole story, you're going to get the person to trust at a level they've never experienced.

"*I NEED TO THINK ABOUT IT*", THE HATED OBJECTION!

Have you ever heard the objection "I need to think about it?" Salespeople normally do not like this objection. They don't like it because they've spent a good deal of time with the prospect to educate them on their product or service. At the end of a 2-hour presentation, the last thing they want to hear from the prospect is "I need to think about it."

The solution is really in the details. Remember at the beginning of this chapter when we talked about discovering the prospect's viewpoint? Part of that is how long they've been thinking about purchasing a product or service like yours.

If you found out that the prospect has been thinking about buying a similar product or service like yours for 6 months or more, this objection is quite easy to handle.

Remind them that they have been thinking about it for 6 months or more and that because you care about them, you want to ensure they get the product at this time. Otherwise, what can happen is that 6 months from now, they will still be thinking…but won't have the benefit of the product or service. If they have been wasting time and money, you can also let them know you care enough about them to ensure they do not lose more time and money by thinking about it for another few months.

Completely eliminating their worries from prior experiences sets you up very nicely to bring your prospect into the next step.

8

ENVISIONING
THE FUTURE

GOALS AND DREAMS

Having exhausted the prospect's bad experiences of the past, and having strengthened trust, you can begin having them look at the future.

Now you have to ask them, and be sincerely interested: Where do they want to go? What do they want to create? What are their goals? What are their dreams? What are they really trying to do?

Part of the Education step, down the line, is going to be really educating the prospect on how your product or service supports their goals, dreams, and future vision. In order to do that, you really have to understand what they're thinking. Again, it takes interest and patience to really get the prospect to think about these questions and give you honest answers.

An interesting aspect of this is that most people have not been asked such questions in a long time. Initially, they may be surprised that you're that interested, and the fact that you would be that interested only strengthens the level of trust you've already established.

STAY INTERESTED ENOUGH TO FIND THE VITAL DETAILS

One of the issues we discover with inconsistent salespeople is when we ask them, "Have you found out the goals and dreams of the prospect?" they'll almost always answer, "Yes, yes!" But there are no details.

Details are vital. When the prospect tells you all about their interests, problems, goals, and dreams, many times they're seeing them for the first time themselves. They've never really worked them out. They're working them out while they're telling you about it. For the prospect, telling you about their goals, dreams, and visions is quite therapeutic. For that reason, the details are extremely important. We must note here that this is a vital skill. One the top 20% salesperson applies.

Let's just take a goal like a vacation, the prospect tells you they've always wanted to go to Rome. Many times a salesperson, being told this, would simply answer, "That's pretty cool!" and carry on with the pitch. Actually, there should be an immediate follow-up question such as "Why? What's your interest in going to Rome? Have you been there before? What do you know about it?" You might discover that they're Italian and their family heritage traces back to Rome, and they've been dreaming their whole life of going there. Once again, how long have they been thinking about it? This would all be part of the details you want to get. The vacation turns into a whole picture of exactly why they want to go.

You might also want to find out what has prevented them from going to Rome. Why haven't they ever done this? That's part of the detail, too. If your product or service can help them achieve this particular goal, that makes your later Education step that much stronger.

Another great example of envisioning the future: A lot of people will say they want to make a lot of money, or they want to "make a million dollars." Again, the key is in the details. The follow-up question to such a statement would be, "What are you going to do when you get that money?" Or, even better, "When you get that money, how will it change your life? What are you going to do differently?"

Such questions open up a whole bunch of detail they haven't even figured out yet. Maybe they've only figured out that they want to make a lot of money, but they've never worked out what they're going to do with it. You are helping them to clearly see their own goals and with this clarity, their motivation to take action is increased!

THE WHOLE PICTURE BECOMES CLEAR

This line of questioning becomes critical to the whole picture and the fact that you would take the time to ask and be interested always strengthens the relationship. At this point in the sales process, you have already developed trust; all you're doing now is making it stronger, which you will continue to do throughout the rest of the sales process.

By the time you arrive at the close, the prospect really feels like they're buying from a friend. That's a whole different point of view from traditional sales, isn't it?

AN UNBREAKABLE, LIFELONG RELATIONSHIP

Once again, this comes back to the point that when you first meet the prospect, you should approach them as though they're going to be a client for life. You don't have a lifelong relationship with a mere acquaintance, you have a lifelong relationship with a friend.

Throughout the sales process, you're developing that relationship. By the time we get to ask about the prospect's future vision, goals, and dreams, we have a nice solid relationship that is now just being strengthened.

It's a relationship you really need to care for. The key points are being interested, fully understanding, and asking more questions. If you don't understand something, ask more questions. Care enough to truly understand your friend and/or client's viewpoint.

At this point, if you've done a really great job, that relationship is unbreakable. That means your competition can't break it, nor can anything else. You're totally ready for the up-front agreement.

9

THE UP-FRONT AGREEMENT

Now we come to the stage where you're going to get the prospect's agreement to buy. As long as you present a solution that truly supports their goals and dreams, solves their problems while saving them time and money, and helps them make money, you'll have no problem getting an upfront agreement that the prospect would be willing to look over. If you know how to work and achieve each of the previous steps, you'll be able to easily obtain that agreement.

At this stage, you can also work out any outstanding issues such as budget, the buying process, other decision-makers, or logistics.

THE COLUMBO CLOSE -
A TRIBUTE TO THE MASTER

You can take a bit of a humorous approach to the up-front agreement, which is something we do all the time at SELL-ability. One of our favorite actors, while we were growing up, was Peter Falk, especially Peter Falk as the title character in the TV show *Columbo*.

In the TV show, Columbo was a disheveled, disorganized detective whom nobody thought much of. He'd be casually questioning the criminal or the murderer and they wouldn't feel very threatened by him as he appeared to not really know what he was doing. Just when they thought he was done questioning them, and he was about to leave, he'd turn back and say, "Oh, I almost forgot. One last thing." He'd then drop

the crucial question, and the criminal or murderer would be trapped because they had totally let their guard down. It was the easiest time to ask the most important question.

A salesperson can take a similar approach. Having done all the work of the previous steps, the salesperson could say, "Oh, I almost forgot. What's your budget for that?" Or, "I forgot to ask, and my boss will kill me if I don't find out. What's your buying process? How do you normally make a decision on a purchase like this?"

Now we make our way through the short remainder of the sales process and to success!

10

SUMMARY OF EDUCATION, AGREEMENT, AND CLOSING

EDUCATION STEP

As you have probably figured out, the Education step boils down to utilizing all you've learned from each of the prior steps. It's all used to educate the prospect on how your product or service is going to support them.

Education is done very precisely, based on the prospect's point of view. The relationship we have worked so hard to develop is now capable of being a lifelong relationship. The Education step must prove how you're going to help the prospect achieve everything they've communicated to you up to this point. You're not only going to deliver on that, but you're also going to deliver more than they expected.

The end result of the Education step is trust, further strengthened by a solution that's going to do exactly what they need it to, and even more. Precisely what the prospect wanted and then some.

The Education step, in reality, is extremely short and becomes a very interesting presentation for the prospect. Up to this point, the prospect has done most of the talking. At this stage, the prospect is really anticipating the solution. They know it's coming because you've done such a great job of setting it up. They've been so well taken care of that they are, in fact, already thinking about how to buy the product or service.

ALL YOU KNOW FROM THE PROSPECT'S POINT OF VIEW... AND NO MORE

You don't want to violate the incredible trust you've created by educating the prospect on anything other than what you've actually found out from them. Take those elements, use them, and enhance them. Remember that everything you educate the prospect about is going to support the solution for them.

Once you've completed the Education step, the prospect is going to be inspired to take action. They won't even be thinking about the competition. At that point, there will be an easy transition to the Agreement stage because the Education has been so strong.

PREPARATION IS CRUCIAL
BEFORE EDUCATION

One action you want to make sure you take before you make your presentation in the Education step is to thoroughly review your presentation from the viewpoint of the prospect. Take everything you've now learned and look at your presentation as though you were the prospect. You basically become your prospect and do your presentation.

If you were the prospect and you were seeing this presentation, would it address all of your concerns? Would it satisfy your problems, goals, and dreams? Would you be excited and inspired to take action?

A true professional drills their presentation beforehand, not only to ensure that it addresses all the prospect's concerns,

A true professional drills their presentation and reads their email and communication, caring for the client's viewpoint before they hit send.

but also that it really cares for the relationship. Make sure you have missed nothing.

If you really do this step well, your prospect will certainly be inspired to take action. The Agreement step will come easy and Closing will be no more than logistics—working out the paperwork, contract, and those sorts of things.

OBJECTIONS DURING AGREEMENT

Now, what happens if you get objections during the Agreement step? If you have really done your work well on all the prior steps, it's actually realistic that you won't get any objections at this point. But, remember that a sale is reactive, not logical, so there may be a bit of sales resistance left in the prospect.

If you do get an objection, simply listen, understand, and acknowledge it. Then you can remind the prospect why they should move forward—*from their own point of view, using all the information you learned from them during the sales process.* Remember, the prospect cannot argue with their own viewpoint. They can, however, argue with the salesperson's point of view!

FINAL WORD ON SKIPPING STEPS IN THE SALES PROCESS

By now, we are pretty sure you are very motivated to closely follow the steps of the sales process. As a final reminder, this is what happens when the steps are skipped:

The prospect gets an idea of your product or service and starts to think about it. During this time, the prospect starts to do research. This research can be from the internet, friends, or other sources. The information from these sources potentially contains opinions, false data, lies, competitive advice, incorrect ideas *or* truth, facts, accurate data, and valuable information. The prospect, at best, has 50% of the information needed to make the best decision. This research takes time. It could be months or years until they reach out to your company and start the sales process.

At this point, they are dragging all of that research (some good, some bad) with them into your sales process. The prospect is also dragging along all of their prior bad experiences with buying and salespeople. All of the resistance that has built up over time; the objections they have successfully used in the past. All of this baggage comes with the prospect into the sales process.

By following the sales process step-by-step, this resistance, past experiences, and objections melt away. All of the questions are professionally answered throughout the process and at the end, we are left with a simple Closing step that consists of finalizing the paperwork and achieving an exchange where both parties win.

By skipping the steps of the sales process, the prospect continues to drag all of that baggage of unhandled resistance and questions with them to the close. This forces the salesperson to try to handle the entire package of resistance at the close. Most of the time this will be unsuccessful. Note, that if the customer is dragging this resistance with them, they are never truly paying attention during the process. Their attention is on their past experience and not with you!

Master the sales process and master closing!

AFTERWORD

We hope you have really enjoyed the book and have already put it to good use! We wrote it for you to *use* and hope you take that to heart. Solving the 80/20 problem requires that you implement a continuous improvement and maintenance system for your sales program.

This system includes, in sequence, the following steps:

1. **Sales Process:** This is the core, the foundation. You must study and *know* it. Customize it as needed to fit your company. Then, drill and practice each step. Practice is ideally done daily and weekly. If you need help, use the online system for drilling. There are hundreds of drills being added to the SELLability library all the time. You can also contact us, we have an abundance of experience creating sales processes all over the world.

2. **Core Abilities:** These are the abilities you will need in order to effectively get your prospects through the sales process. This category also includes marketing and sales

collateral (materials) that follow the sales process and provide critical support as the salesperson guides the prospect through the process. Again, if you need help with the design or creation of these materials or tools, contact us.

3. **The Rule of 8:** These 8 steps are provided in detail because they are so critical for success, from the beginning of the sales process through the completion of the Qualify step. We found these steps to be the weakest part of the sales process for most salespeople and the key reason for low closing rates. Again, we must emphasize the need to practice and drill the Rule of 8.

All aspects of this book are very well covered on videos with drills and exercises as part of the SELLability online sales training program.

NEXT STEPS

1. Finish reading this book if you haven't already done so.
2. Visit SELLability.com and take the Sales Skills Assessment test, based on the 8 Core Abilities. Once you have completed your test, you will receive a graph showing your strengths and weaknesses in these 8 Core Abilities.
3. Become a SELLability member at *www.SELLability.com*
4. As a SELLability member, you will receive an individualized online training program, just for you, designed to help you greatly improve and become a top salesperson.
5. Do your SELLability online training program throughout the week and practice, practice, practice.
6. Use the Sales CPR Lifeline for help with your slowed or stuck sales. We call it Sales CPR and believe that your sales are only mostly dead, not *all* dead! Revive them with Sales CPR!
7. Sign up for the SELLability Newsletters which are packed with very useful sales knowledge designed to help you improve your sales abilities throughout the entire sales process.
8. Attend SELLability webinars for real information you can actually put to use immediately to increase your numbers.

FINAL WORD

We are dedicated to helping individuals around the world confidently and competently sell themselves, their ideas, visions, dreams, products, or services and positively impact themselves, their families, their associates, and company, and thereby the overall economy.

This dedication came from our research into the 80/20 problem. Our intention is that you are now empowered to solve the 80/20 problem in your company. We have dedicated 2 companies and thousands of hours of research based on our combined 50 years of experience to bring you what most agree is the holy grail of sales technology.

When this book is studied and used along with the SELL-ability online sales training program, it has been proven time and again that you and your team can get more consistent results, eliminating the traditional sales rollercoaster that is so common.

A modern sales program must provide a simple, proven technology that everyone can learn and apply. With thousands of international sales teams using this technology in 27 countries, SELLability is impacting what we feel is one of the most important professions in the world. Be proud to be a salesperson! Remember that it is the one profession *no company can do without.* If you can become a top professional salesperson, you'll be internationally vital to every economy.

Happy selling!

Scan the QR code below to go to *www.SELLability.com* and take your Sales Skills Assessment Test now!

Before you go, can I ask you for a quick favor?

I hope you enjoyed reading Closing is NOT your problem! Your feedback is important to us and other potential readers. If you can take a moment (I promise it will be quick), we'd greatly appreciate it if you could share your thoughts by leaving a review on Amazon and Goodreads. Your honest review will help others to discover and enjoy this book as well.

To leave a review, simply visit the Amazon page for Closing is NOT your problem! and click on the "Write a Customer Review" button. Or you can scan the QR code below and it will take you right to the place to leave a review.

We are excited to hear what you think and thank you for your support!

With sincere gratitude,

Lisa & Nick Terrenzi

As you continue on this journey into the world of sales strategies and tactics, we invite you to explore more insights and knowledge from our Sales Killers Series. Each book in the series will help you and your team to enhance your skills. Whether you're looking to master the art and skill of negotiation, enhance your communication skills, close deals with finesse, manage a team of sales professionals and more, our series has something for every professional.

SALES KILLERS SERIES:

SALES CPR: 101 SYMPTOMS OF SALES FAILURE AND THEIR SOLUTIONS!

Buy it now on Amazon

GLOSSARY

80/20 Rule:
1. 80 percent of sales are produced by the top 20 percent of salespeople and executives in most businesses. This is a consistent, common problem.

8 Core Abilities:
1. The 8 consistent, foundational abilities that make the top 20% of salespeople effective at each step of the sales process. These abilities must be known and continually improved in all salespeople. They are: 1. Communication 2. Control 3. Contact 4. Certainty 5. Confidence 6. Competence 7. Closing 8. Customer Relationship Also see: Core Ability

8 Cs of Selling:
SELLability's 8 Core abilities- "C" = Core

A

Abundance:
1. A great or plentiful amount
2. The condition of being rich in supply

Administration:

1. The process or activity of running a business, organization, etc.

Affluent:

1. Having a great deal of money; wealthy.

Agreement:

1. Harmony or accordance in opinion or feeling; a position or result of agreeing.

2. A negotiated and typically legally binding arrangement between parties as to a course of action.

Agreement step:

1. The customer has firmly decided to buy and has voiced that decision.

Arrogance:

1. Offensive display of superiority or self-importance; overbearing pride

B

Biographical:

1. Dealing with a particular person's life.

Burn out:

1. Ruin one's health or become completely exhausted through overwork. In sales, burnout is largely caused by an imbalance of sales failures vs sales successes.

C

Closing step:

1. The successful transition of the prospect from the salesperson to the delivery team. Includes all paperwork being completed with signatures and properly routed. This frees up the salesperson to completely focus on the sales process with another customer. Attention is no longer tied up in the worry of whether or not the previous customer will be taken care of.

Certainty:

1. Knowing as much as possible about your prospect, their company, and their line of products and services.

2. Without doubt

3. Firm conviction that something is the case.

4. It is the salesperson who knows their product or service flawlessly and knows how to handle prospect resistance. They are also totally professional and are masters of their company's sales process.

Collateral:

1. Any media, print or digital, that makes a strong case for your product or service. Collateral is used to help salespeople have consistent, effective presentations.

Columbo Close:

1. The name of the Columbo Close originates from the TV show Columbo, which aired throughout the 1970s. The show was about a detective named Columbo, who roamed the streets of Los Angeles, catching criminals. A cunning and clever man, Columbo didn't get easily outwitted by the criminals he was chasing. He would casually question the criminal or the murderer and they wouldn't feel very threatened by him as he appeared to not really know what he was doing. Just when they thought he was done questioning them, and he was about to leave, he'd turn back and say, "Oh, I almost forgot.

One last thing." He'd then drop the crucial question, and the criminal or murderer would be trapped (closed) because they had totally let their guard down.

Competent:

1. Having the necessary ability, knowledge, or skill to do something successfully.

2. Efficient and capable.

Conceptual:

1. Relating to or based on mental concepts. Dealing with or expressing a quality or idea.

Conduct:

1. The manner in which a person behaves, especially on a particular occasion or in a particular context.

Confidence:

1. The feeling or belief that one can rely on someone or something; firm trust.

2. A feeling of self-assurance arising from one's appreciation of one's own abilities or qualities.

3. A belief or certainty that an outcome will be favorable:

4. In sales Confidence means that the salesperson totally understands each step of the sales process and the 8 core abilities required to successfully guide the prospect through the process. Confidence means the salesperson understands the prospects' emotions and understands that the prospect probably had previous bad buying experiences, which causes resistance to the sales process.

Contact and Interview steps:

1. You've established *real* communication not just social in the contact step starting to strengthen the customers' trust and through the interview step, further developed enough trust that your prospect is willing to disclose to you what they are truly thinking. Achieving this will then lead to a successful Qualifying step.

Controversial:

1. Giving rise or likely to give rise to public disagreement.

Convey:

1. Make (an idea, impression, or feeling) known or understandable to someone.

2. Communicate (a message or information).

Conversely:

1. Introducing a statement or idea which reverses one that has just been made or referred to.

Core Ability:

1. The central or most important part of talent, skill, or proficiency in a particular area.

In SELLability: The 8 consistent, foundational abilities that make the top 20% of salespeople effective at each step of the sales process. These abilities must be known and continually improved in all salespeople. They are: 1. Communication 2. Control 3. Contact 4. Certainty 5. Confidence 6. Competence 7. Closing 8. Customer Relationship

Courteous:

1. Polite, respectful, or considerate in manner.

CRM:
1. Customer Relationship Management software denoting strategies and software that enable a company to organize and optimize its customer relations.

Crunchbase:
1. Crunchbase is a website where you can get the leading destination for company insights from early-stage startups to the Fortune 1000 and insights into your competition.

D

Define:
1. To fix or lay down clearly and definitely; specify distinctly:

Disgruntled:
1. Angry or dissatisfied.

Doubleday Doran:
1. Doubleday is an American publishing company. It was founded as the Doubleday & McClure Company in 1897 and was the largest in the United States by 1947. It published the work of mostly U.S. authors under a number of imprints and distributed them through its own stores.

Dominant personality:
1. This personality type is described as task-oriented, rather than people-oriented, and is generally characterized as direct, decisive, and highly self-confident.

E

Education Step:
1. Is a laser-precise process that educates the prospect based *exactly* on the interests, needs and wants provided by the

customer in the Qualify step. Critical that we use the information/viewpoint of the customer not the viewpoint of the salesperson.

2. Education includes how your product or service saves that customer time, saves them money, makes them money, solves their problems, and aligns with their goals All of this education is based on the trustable information obtained in the Qualify step.

3. Education Result: The customer knows that your product or service will exceed their expectations, they disregard the competition and the customer is inspired to take action to obtain your product or service.

Elevator pitch:

1. A briefly and clearly expressed persuasive sales pitch. Also commonly referred to as your "USP" unique selling proposition. The idea is that you would be able to give an informative and effective sales pitch in the time it takes to go down the elevator with someone (in under a minute).

Embracive:

1. Inclusive, comprehensive

Err:

1. Be mistaken or incorrect; make a mistake.

etiquette [ˈɛtɪˌkɛt ˌɛtɪˈkɛt] *n*

1. *The rules indicating the proper and polite way to behave (including appearance)*

2. (Sociology) the customs or rules governing behavior regarded as correct or acceptable in social or official life.

3. (Sociology) a conventional but unwritten code of practice followed by members of any of certain professions or groups. *Collins English Dictionary – Complete and Unabridged* © HarperCollins Publishers 1991, 1994, 1998, 2000, 2003 According to Wikipedia, "**Etiquette** is a code of behavior that delineates expectations for social behavior according to contemporary conventional norms within a society, social class, or group."

F

Flow:

1. The action or fact of moving along in a steady, continuous stream.

2. Sales flow: Sequence of actions leading to results at each step of the sales process moving along a path to the close.

Fortune 100 and Fortune 500:

1. The Fortune 100 is a list of the top 100 companies in the United States. It is a subset of the Fortune 500, a list of the 500 largest U.S. public and privately held companies published by Fortune magazine. Fortune creates the list by ranking public and private companies that report annual revenue figures to a government agency.

Foundation:

1. An underlying basis or principle.

G

Genuine:

1. Truly what something is said to be; authentic.

2. (Of a person, emotion, or action) sincere.

Grant:

1. You give or accord

Grant Importance:

1. You give importance to another. Recognize another as important. Some actions you can do to grant importance to another are: Pay attention to them, listen to what they are saying, acknowledge them throughout the conversation to let them know you heard what they said. Make them the priority over everything else (phones, computers, etc).

Guru:

1. An influential teacher or popular expert.

H

Holy grail:

1. A thing that is being earnestly pursued or sought after.

HP:

1. HP is identified by Wired magazine as the producer of the world's first device to be called a personal computer: the Hewlett-Packard 9100A, introduced in 1968.

I

IBM:

1. International Business Machines, a leading US computer manufacturer.

Importance:

1. Social status; standing; esteem: *a man of importance*

Indispensable:

1. Absolutely necessary.

Inevitably:

1. As is certain to happen; unavoidably.

Influx:

1. An arrival or entry of large numbers of people or things.

Interlude:

1. An intervening period of time.

2. A pause between the acts of a play.

Interview:

1. A meeting of people face to face, especially for consultation.

2. Interview step: Through the interview step you further develop enough trust that your prospect is willing to disclose to you what they are truly thinking. Achieving this will then lead to a successful Qualifying step.

K

Key:

1. Crucial importance.

2. In sales: Opening a door to improve your selling skills

L

Logistics:

1. The detailed coordination of a complex operation involving many people, facilities, or supplies.

M

Manners:

1. A socially acceptable way of behaving

2. *Today's Etiquette,* written by Lillian Eichler and published in 1941 by Doubleday Doran: "Good manners are not only indispensable in society, but they have a very practical value in the business world."

Manipulative:

1. Characterized by unscrupulous (unethical) control of a situation or person.

Margins:

1. Profit made on the transaction or sale of a good or service.

Microsoft:

1. Microsoft Corporation is an American multinational technology company with headquarters in Redmond, Washington. It develops, manufactures, licenses, supports, and sells computer software, consumer electronics, personal computers, and related services.

N

New York Times:

1. The New York Times (NYT or NY Times) is an American daily newspaper based in New York City with a worldwide readership. Founded in 1851, the Times has since won 130 Pulitzer Prizes (the most of any newspaper), and has long been regarded within the industry as a national " newspaper of record ".

Numbers Game:

1. The use or manipulation of statistics or figures, especially in support of an argument.

2. In sales: an inefficient way of increasing sales numbers.

O

Over Focus:
1. Hyper focus on a certain interest or activity.

Overemphasis:
1. Excessive emphasis.

P

Pain points:
1. A persistent or recurring problem (as with a product or service) that frequently inconveniences or annoys customers.
2. In sales often referred to as the points powerful enough to cause a customer to purchase a product or service that solves/fixes the pain.

Pareto Principle:
1. There's a rule or law, also known as the Pareto Principle, that states that 80 percent of effects come from 20 percent of the causes. In sales, this rule is modified to state that 80 percent of sales are made by 20 percent of salespeople, which has been observed and written about over the last century.

Pilot phase:
1. The pilot phase or phases are needed to test the project deliverables "in the field" so that when they are released to production, many or all issues have been found and added to the issues log so that they may be rectified by the project's technical working group.

Positive control:
1. Good control used on an individual that is done in a way that the individual is willing to be controlled. In SELLability,

a prospect is guided through the sales process with positive control.

Practical:
1. Of or concerned with the actual doing or use of something rather than with theory and ideas.

Preconceptions:
1. A preconceived idea
2. In sales: Idea that a customer formed based on a past experience bad or good with a similar product or service to yours.

Precisely:
1. In exact terms; without vagueness.
2. Exactly, not vague

Pro Sales Network:
1. SELLability hosts the Pro Sales Network—a membership organization dedicated to helping salespeople conquer all aspects of the entire sales process. Through SELLability and the Pro Sales Network, we create an army of salespeople and organizations using SELLability technologies to greatly and positively affect the overall economy.

Prospect:
1. A person regarded as likely to succeed as a potential customer, client, etc.
2. A potential customer that fits the profile of your target market

Prospecting Result:
1. You've developed a huge database of potential prospects, of the public who will buy your products or services. You

have provided them with valuable free content, keeping them actively in communication with your company, resulting in your company being considered a valuable source of information *and* a company the prospects can *trust!*

Prospecting:

1. Look out for; search for.

2. Searching for potential public/prospects that fit the profile of your target market meaning they would or could purchase your product or service.

Push marketing:

1. Push marketing is a strategy that is used most frequently by start-ups and companies introducing new products into the market. Since the focus is on taking the product to the consumer, it is particularly suited to products that the consumer is not yet aware of. This style of marketing can be used by companies large and small. Example: radio, TV, social media, email, text, billboards, and others

Q

Qualify:

1. Make (someone) competent or knowledgeable enough to do something.

2. In sales: Verifying with that prospect (business or project), that your product or service is truly a match for them. SELL-ability defines "match" as having most of the following points: saving that prospective customer time, saving them money, making them money, solving their problems and supporting their goals.

Qualifying step:
1. Finding out why the prospect should purchase your product or service, from *their* point of view; *not* from the salesperson's point of view! Includes the interests, needs and wants provided by the customer.
2. Working out how your product or service saves that customer time, saves them money, makes them money, solves their problems and aligns with their goals.
3. A true completion of the Qualifying step would provide the salesperson with total certainty needed to educate and transition to agreement and closing steps.

R

Re-engineer:
1. Redesign
2. Restructure

Referrals:
1. An act of referring someone or something for consultation, review, or further action. In SELLability, a true referral includes an introduction and not just a name.

Research step:
1. You've cared enough to establish a foundation of information that is going to allow the Contact and Interview step to go more smoothly. This is going to allow you to develop trust much more efficiently because you are able to use what was learned in research to effectively open communication in the contact step. Eliminates need to "Cold Call".

Respect:
1. The state of being honored or esteemed; edified.

Resistance:
1. The refusal to accept or comply with something; the attempt to prevent something by action or argument.
2. In sales: most prospects resist salespeople and the sales process based on many previous bad buying experiences. Salespeople also resist prospect resistance.

Revenue:
1. Money made by a company; income, especially when of a company or organization and of a substantial nature.

Rodeo Drive:
1. Rodeo Drive is a two-mile-long street, in Beverly Hills, California, with its southern segment in the City of Los Angeles.

Rote:
1. Mechanical or habitual repetition of something to be learned.
2. In sales relates to a scripted process, not well thought of by customers.

Rule of 8:
1. SELLability's Rule of 8 provides you with an 8-step key to getting a prospect talking and unlocking early-stage sales resistance during the steps prior to the Qualify step.

S

Sale:
1. The exchange of goods, services or property for money
2. SELLability defines sales as: an exchange in which both parties win.

Sales CPR:

1. Coined from (Cardio, Pulmonary, Resuscitation). A service SELLability provides to revive dead sales and bring them back to life and eventually close them: Your sales are only "mostly dead" not all dead!

Sales force:

1. The division of a business that's responsible for selling products or services. Evaluating your current sales force is an important step in the process of deciding whether and how to grow your sales team.

Sales management:

1. Sales management is the process of hiring, training and motivating sales staff, coordinating operations across the sales department and implementing a cohesive sales strategy that drives business revenues. Sales are the lifeblood of any organization and managing the sales process is one of the most important functions of any business.

Sales Professionalism:

1. Having the abilities to overcome sales resistance and guide the prospect to the product or service solution that ultimately exceeds their expectations.

Sales Process

1. The fundamental, systematic, repeatable series of steps that map out and track interactions with prospects, from their first point of engagement with you, all the way through to the close.

Sales rollercoaster:
1. The ups and downs of selling - sometimes closing sales, then sometimes failing to close, then closing, then failing etc...

SELLability:
See SELLability Technologies.

SELLability Technologies:
1. SELLability Technologies, LC provides a variety of sales solutions. It's purpose is to greatly increase the number of salespeople who are prospering by increasing their ability to SELL—thus the name, SELLability. Through SELLability, salespeople continuously improve their closing rates and all abilities required to be effective throughout the sales process.

Stark-raving mad:
1. Completely crazy.

Strategic Alliance:
1. A strategic alliance is an arrangement between two companies to undertake a mutually beneficial project while each retains its independence. The agreement is less complex and less binding than a joint venture, in which two businesses combine resources to create a separate business entity.

Statistics:
1. The practice or science of collecting and analyzing numerical data in large quantities, especially for the purpose of inferring proportions in a whole from those in a representative sample.
2. KPIs (Key Performance Indicators). In sales, statistics relates to being able to track results at each step of the sales process. These are measured against time. Some examples include:

Leads, number of prospects, contacts, closes and conversion rates, etc. All for the purpose of managing and continuously improving sales.

Subsequent:

1. Coming after something in time; following.

Surveys:

1. Investigate the opinions or experience of (a group of people) by asking them questions. Also known as Market Research.

T

Target audience:

1. A particular group at which a film, book, advertising campaign, etc., is aimed.

2. In sales the target audience would be clearly defined as the public that is the best match for your products and services and would buy them.

Technology:

1. Making, modification, usage, and knowledge of tools, machines, techniques, crafts, systems and methods of organization.

2. SELLability Technologies focuses on creating technology that effectively increases sales, salespeople, sales management and customer service.

Tenure:

1. The holding of an office for a period of time.

Tone:

1. The general character or attitude of a place, piece of writing, situation, etc. can be positive or negative.

Trial and error:

1. The process of experimenting with various methods of doing something until one finds the most successful pattern of operation.

U

Unique Selling Proposition, or USP:

1. What makes you different? A unique selling proposition, or USP, is a tool used by marketers and salespeople to easily communicate the key factors that differentiate their products and services from the competition.

Unqualified:

1. Not competent or sufficiently knowledgeable to do something.

2. In sales: a prospect that is not a match for your products or services.

V

Validate:

1. Check or prove the validity or accuracy of (something).

Verbatim:

1. In exactly the same words as were used originally.

W

Winging:

1. Speak or act without preparation; improvise.

INDEX

Made in the USA
Las Vegas, NV
11 January 2024

84220791R00144